THE SPIRIT OF
CHURCH HISTORY

THE SPIRIT OF CHURCH HISTORY

BY

J. W. C. WAND

Lord Bishop of London

A. R. MOWBRAY & Co. LIMITED
LONDON AND OXFORD
MOREHOUSE GORHAM CO.
NEW YORK

First published in 1947

PRINTED IN GREAT BRITAIN BY
A. R. MOWBRAY & Co. LIMITED, LONDON AND OXFORD
7486

PREFACE

THESE Lectures were delivered in the Hall of Holy Trinity Church, Kingsway, during the Lent of 1947 at the invitation of the Adult Education Committee of the London Diocesan Board of Education. They were originally intended for clergy, but the laity gate-crashed the proceedings at the start and continued to form a large proportion of the audience. Their presence explains to some extent the line of treatment actually followed.

The talks were delivered extempore from a bare analysis without notes. A stenographer was in attendance, and the text represents her report. I have removed some of the more detestable enormities of the spoken word. I have not, however, toned down either the directness of address or the repetitiveness which are part of the technique of a platform lecturer. Even my riposte to the gust of laughter aroused by the mention of Henry VIII remains on record.

I am grateful both to those whose encouragement has led to the reproduction of the Lectures in permanent form, and also to those whose kind hospitality made it possible to combine a Lenten penance with a pleasing social event.

✠ WM: LONDIN:

CONTENTS

CONTENTS

THE SPIRIT OF
CHURCH HISTORY

I

THE FOUNDATION

MAY I begin by saying a word about the purpose and scope of these five Lenten Lectures. They were originally intended as a Refresher Course for the Clergy; and a Refresher Course implies that there will be nothing new in them; that they are simply intended to refresh your memory, to remind you of things that you learned long ago. There may be some value in trying to take a bird's-eye view of a vast subject; it will enable one the better to see the wood for the trees. I personally was glad when I later learnt that some of our laity were going to be present. It is possible that they may sometimes find that I talk about things in a way which is unexpected to them. They will realize, of course, that I cannot stop to give evidence for every particular statement, or point of view, in a series of lectures of this kind. They must rest in the belief that there *is* evidence for what I have to say.

We must begin by establishing the fact that the

Church has a right to its existence. There are people, of course, who try to separate between Christianity and the Church; they say they can put up very well with Christianity, but that they cannot do with the Church.

Documents

Every historian is anxious to get back to his documents; and we must begin by getting back to ours. Our foundation documents are to be found in the New Testament. An interesting thing is that the Church is the very first thing to be mentioned in the New Testament; I mean the first thing historically. The clergy will know that the Gospels are not the earliest part of the New Testament. The earliest part of the New Testament is to be found in the writings of St. Paul. If you take the earliest of his Epistles—the First Epistle to the Thessalonians—what is the first thing you read? 'Paul, and Silvanus, and Timotheus, unto the church of the Thessalonians.' In the historical opening of the New Testament the Church is there at the very beginning. And if you read on to the Epistle to the Galatians you will find there a Letter addressed to the 'churches of Galatia.' There is in a particular place, a particular area, a church, or a number of churches, but behind them, and pervading all the Epistles, was the idea of a great general Church, a Universal Church, of which these local churches are but miniature examples.

You may say, What about the other books of the

New Testament? Have they nothing to do with the Church? Most decidedly they have. If you turn to the Gospels, and ask yourself, What are these Gospels for? the answer is at once forthcoming—they are the handbooks for the use of those who were expanding the Church; they were the handbooks put into the possession of the evangelists who went out to preach the Gospel. They were documents to which reference could be made as evidence for the statements that were handed on by the preachers of the Gospel. Again, the volume known as the Acts of the Apostles tells the story of the early expansion. And still again, if you turn to the Book of the Revelation you will see that that Book tears away the veil from eternity, and reveals the Church in Heaven. It is still a Book quite definitely on and for the Church. It would be right, then, to say that the Church is an all-pervasive idea of the whole of the New Testament from cover to cover.

The Foundation

As historians, where shall we look for its foundation? Of course, in Sunday Schools we teach our children that the birthday of the Christian Church was the first Whit-Sunday; and that is a good answer to give; as good an answer as one could possibly give to children; but it is not a sufficient answer for the scholar. If you study the Epistles of St. Paul, and the other writers, you find that when referring to the institution of the Church they speak of a Person named Jesus, and the whole thing is built up on Him. He is described as the foundation, and the corner-stone. It must be borne in mind that St. Paul is only looking back over a period of about twenty-two or twenty-three years. It is as if a person at the beginning of the second World War looked back to the first World War, and described what he remembered, or knew of the instances connected with it. The memory of the Lord Jesus was quite clear in the minds of those responsible for the earliest books in the New Testament (whether St. Paul knew Him personally or not), and He is the corner-stone of the Church. If, however, you turn to the Old Testament you find that, as a matter of fact, there is a Church before the life of our Lord Himself. The Church does not begin with Jesus Christ. There is a Church of the Old Testament, as well as of the New. There is a Church which goes right back, at least in the idea of the Jewish people, to the Covenant that God made with Abraham, a Church which is co-extensive with the Jewish nation; that is to say, a nation and Church which are two aspects of the same entity.

When the New Testament opens there is going on in this Old Testament Church a reformation, a reformation which is being preached by none other than John the Baptist. The points of his revelation are that the long-expected Messianic kingdom is about to be set up, and the preparation, prior to entering into it, has begun. That preparation was to get rid of one's sins; and the symbol of the washing away of sin was to be found in baptism. That was the reformation within

the Jewish Church which was going on when our Lord
first appears on the stage of history. He identifies
Himself with that reformation, and quite evidently
He is prepared to assist in the renewal of the Jewish
Church. Presently those associated with Him take
the lead in the reforming movement. And when
they are brought to recognize His own particular
character, nature, and Person, as indicating the Messiah,
the Son of the Living God, He says it is on that rock
that He will build His Church—'My Church.'

There is, then, here a new start in the history of the
one Church that has gone on continuously from the
beginning of revealed religion. It has been launched
on a new era in, and through, the Person of Jesus
Christ; and those whom Christ identifies with Himself are the beginning of a new Israel, a reformation
of the old Church which, as we shall see presently,
is more and more to manifest itself as a new Church.
That, then, is the foundation of the Christian
Church.

The Church existed for some time in this new form
before it was clearly discernible as a distinct organization to the outsider. I think if one had lived in the days
immediately succeeding the Ascension of our Lord
into Heaven, and the descent of the Holy Spirit, one
would not very easily have found the Christians.
Many of them would have been driven into the back
streets of Jerusalem, and into the less-known by-ways
of Palestine. They were distinguished by those who
did get to know them through the fact that they had

continued John the Baptist's ceremonial use of Baptism. They were distinguished also by the fact that they accepted Jesus as the Messiah; and that they met together regularly to take part in a rite which He Himself had instituted, namely, the Lord's Supper, a rite which was, like the Church itself, not a new rite historically conceived, but a new edition, so to speak, of an old rite. These, then, would be the distinctive marks of the Christians everywhere, but they would not be easily discernible by those who did not understand their secret.

Separation

One of the most interesting elements in the early history of the Christian Church is the way in which it disentangled itself from its surroundings, and became more and more clearly a separate entity. I want to dwell for a few minutes on this separation, because it was in the course of it that the Church went through the greatest of all the struggles that it has ever had to face. We sometimes think we have difficult periods in our own day. We read back in the history of various epochs, and we sometimes commiserate the Christians of those days upon the difficulties they had to face. But never in the whole course of the Church's history has there been so difficult a phase as that which faced it at the outset of its career.

The reasons are fairly obvious. Hitherto, those who were members of the Christian Church were also members of the Jewish race and the Jewish Church.

The distinctive mark of the membership of the Jewish race, and of the Jewish Church, was circumcision. And through that initiation every Jew had to enter the Church. If Gentiles, or people of non-Jewish race, wished to become members of it, they had to adopt the same method. If they were not willing to take that very strong step, they had to remain as proselytes at the gates of Judaism, not being full members of the Jewish Church, but nevertheless trying to enjoy what they could of the fruits of its exalted morality, with its definite monotheistic teaching. At first this was also true if they wished to become members of the Christian Church. The Christian Church itself was a kind of enclave within Judaism, a small, select body of specially holy people with particular ideas, and, as I have pointed out, with certain distinctive marks of their own. They were a body enclosed within a much larger circle, that of Judaism, and consequently to be a Christian you must first become a Jew.

The first great crisis of the Christian Church comes in the disentanglement of the Christian Church from the Jewish Church, and the setting it upon a course of its own. The possibility was first discussed among the officials who had been called in to assist the apostles in the administration of charitable funds in Jerusalem. The people who had complained that their widows were neglected were members of the Jewish Dispersion; and the officers who were appointed to assist the apostles belonged to the same circle. It was in that

B

circle that dislike of the contemporary organization first began to manifest itself.

It was shown, first of all, in the preaching of St. Stephen. Stephen proclaimed that Judaism was not, as a matter of fact, the last word; but that there had been a new revelation, which superseded the old. For that teaching he was put to death. One of his colleagues, Philip, went still further, and acted upon the kind of teaching that Stephen was giving. He even went so far as to baptize the Ethiopian eunuch, a man whose very condition made it impossible for him to be a full member of the Jewish Church. Not only so, but he baptized certain Samaritans who were at such feuds with the Jews that they would not have been accepted as members of the Jewish Church. Here already there is beginning to be a break between Christianity and the Judaism in which it had been set.

Presently St. Peter was drawn into the movement by an extraordinary happening at Joppa. I imagine that as he had been looking out over the sea, watching the ships with their brown sails passing by, he had fallen asleep. Perhaps he had been meditating upon the situation now arising between Christianity and Judaism. At any rate, in his dream he sees the sail of one of those ships let down, as it were from heaven, filled with all manner of beasts, clean and unclean, and he is commanded to 'take and eat.' He revolts at the idea. 'I have never eaten anything that is common, or unclean,' he says. When he awakes from his sleep he finds the messengers from Cornelius. They are not Jews, but uncircumcised proselytes 'of the gate.' Yet when St. Peter began to teach them about Christianity he found that they manifested the same ecstatic qualities and tokens of the descent of the Holy Spirit as the original disciples themselves manifested on the day of Pentecost. St. Peter realizes that something quite extraordinary has happened to them. He would have been the last person to introduce uncircumcised proselytes into the Christian Church. But reflection on the meaning of his dream makes him feel that here is the call of God actually to baptize these people; and so he takes the quite decisive step of admitting converts who have not gone through the gate of Judaism into full membership of the Church.

Then, on top of that, there comes the final step taken by St. Paul. He had heard the preaching of Stephen; he had been led under the influence of that preaching, brought home to him by his experience on the Damascus road, to abandon his life as a persecutor, to accept the claims of Jesus, and to ask for membership in the Christian Church. To him as he looks back the whole secret of history is revealed in the breaking down of the barrier between Jew and Gentile. In Christ every barrier has been broken down; men of all kinds have been united; and, in the face of that, there can be no further insistence upon what now seemed to him to be a barbarous rite, that of circumcision. If there were Jews who wanted to continue in that way, let them; but they had no right to try and enforce anything of the kind on Gentiles who wished to come into the Christian Church. Thus the whole of the Jewish initiation is swept away, and the new Christian initiation is regarded as entirely sufficient for introduction into the Christian Church. Henceforth membership of the Christian Church comes by baptism, and by the gift of the Holy Spirit. Nothing further is asked except faith.

That is the story of the separation of the new Christian Church from the old Jewish Church. The jewel has come out of its setting; it now has a separate existence of its own.

Organization

Having thus seen the Christian Church launched on its independent career, let us ask ourselves how it was organized. And here I would like to say a preliminary word. In the providence of God, these happenings took place at a time when it was possible for the new Church to receive a great deal of help from the interaction of different racial and national forces. It is well-known that the influence of Greek philosophy was still very strongly felt throughout the whole of the civilized world. It had put questionings in the minds of men, so that they were not prepared to accept things easily on authority, but expected to examine the reason for every position that was taken up. This was a great advantage to the new Church which was just beginning to claim attention. Also, of course, the Greek language had spread through the whole of the civilized world, and, although it did not displace Latin it became the *lingua franca* of the period, and was used in business, and in society. Side by side with the Greek influence there was the Roman influence. Rome had made itself mistress of the world of that day; it had organized that world physically more perfectly than it has ever been organized since. It had driven roads from Carlisle to the Nile, and beyond; and it was possible to travel along those roads with the same security as one would have in travelling through English roads to-day. Posts had been organized. Even relays of horses were available under the imperial system, and it was almost as safe for St. Paul to post his letters as it is for us to-day. Thus from the Greek and the Roman side there were great forces assisting the spread of the Christian Church.

Sometimes it has been suggested that the new Church was tremendously influenced by this Græco-Roman environment. When I was a young man it was the custom for scholars to try and derive as many of the Christian institutions as they possibly could from Græco-Roman society. I have lived long enough to see an extraordinary swing of the pendulum. We have begun to feel that nearly every Christian institution can find its origin, not in the Græco-Roman environment, but in the Jewish environment, and in the course of what I have to say now that will become fairly clear.

Sunday

A new movement may be influenced by its environment in two directions. It may borrow a great deal from that environment, or it may react violently against it. In the case of the first institution I wish to mention the influence is rather by way of violent reaction. I refer to the observance of Sunday. I suppose there is hardly any step the Church has ever taken which has shown its belief in its own power, and its responsibility for its own administration so clearly as the change-over from the Jewish Sabbath to the Christian Sunday. It is a thousand pities that people will talk about the Christian Sunday as the Sabbath, because it obscures the whole historical development. Actually the Christian Sunday and the Jewish Sabbath existed side by side, as they do still. Sunday had nothing whatever to do with the Sabbath. The Christian Jews observed their Sabbath like their fellow countrymen; but, in addition, they began also to observe the day of the week on which their Saviour rose from the dead, and very early that day became the Lord's Day set aside for special observance. But its observance was not at all like that of the Sabbath. The observance of the Sabbath was largely that of taboos. The emphasis of the Christian Sunday was on the positive, and not on the negative aspect of a holy day. Worship formed the essential part of the observance of the Christian Sunday, and there was the repetition of that rite which the Lord had instituted, the Lord's Supper. Each Lord's Day it was regularly observed, and coming on the first day of the week I think it would be the most obvious observance by which the Christians could be clearly distinguished from their Jewish neighbours.

The Scriptures

Side by side with the Sunday we have to notice the institution of the Scriptures. The Christian Church, of course, took over the Jewish Scriptures; it used them; it did not reject them, as you might easily have thought it would when it found itself in violent opposition to the bulk of the Jewish people. When the Christian Church found that it could not win over the Jewish race as a whole, it might very well have said, We will have nothing whatever to do with the things which the Jewish people treasure. On the contrary, it accepted the Old Testament Scriptures; it even used them against the Jews by saying, As a matter of fact these Scriptures are fulfilled in us, in our Church. And, in order to show that fulfilment, they began to put side by side with the old Jewish Scriptures new Scriptures of their own. I imagine they began to do so as a practical matter rather than as a symbolical gesture. When St. Paul sent his Letters to a particular Church, those Letters were read out to the congregation in the course of the ordinary meeting for worship; and when the Old Testament Scriptures were read St. Paul's Letters would find a place side by side with them as being of importance to the congregation. By reason of their collocation, St. Paul's Letters would receive a definitely sacred character, because such Letters were read at the same time, and in the same service, as the Old Testament Scriptures; and there would, therefore, be given to the New Testament writings, the writings of the Christian Church, something of the same sacred character as belonged already to the Old Testament Scriptures. Gradually there would be formed a corpus of such new scriptures, and they would be regarded as worthy of being placed side by side with the old scriptures as having some sort of apostolic origin; the apostles being regarded as of at least equal importance with the prophets.

At the same time there was going on a development in the building up of a canon of information with regard to the life of Christ. I have already said that the Gospels were actually missioners' handbooks. They began as oral narratives; a teacher wanted to tell his class about the Christ; to repeat some story that Christ Himself had told; or he would narrate one of the miracles which Christ had wrought, or he would try to remember what he could of some conversation, or argument which Christ had had with the Scribes and Pharisees; and he would try to work the thing up to some definite point. All these small pieces of information about Christ would be repeated, in the characteristic Eastern fashion over and over again, until both teacher and class knew them by heart. I think that is the real secret of the oral origin of the Scriptures. I remember when I was a boy people used to think that, somehow, it would be possible for a Jewish teacher to remember a whole Gospel, and to repeat it by heart. We used to be told of the extraordinary memories these Eastern people had. They certainly must have been very extraordinary indeed if they repeated whole Gospels by heart. I, personally, very much prefer to think in the more modern terms, not of a whole Gospel as the unit of repetition, but of a particular narrative, argument or parable. You can imagine an Eastern teacher sitting before his class, and repeating a narrative over and over again until it gets into a fixed form of words, and commits itself to the memory. Well, now, by degrees there would be a whole collection of these oral pieces about the life and teaching of Christ. Then some one comes along, and begins to put together the little repertoire in writing. Presently there would be a number of manuscripts; one manuscript, perhaps, describing the teaching of Christ; another describing His life and work. There must have been a considerable number of such manuscripts. I feel quite certain that one of them quite regularly used by the Christian teachers must have been a manuscript giving a number of texts from the Old Testament, proving that the Jewish scriptures pointed to Jesus as the Messiah. The Gospels, as we have them to-day, are a compilation of such manuscripts. Some of the evangelists used the same documents, but each of them had individual sources of his own on which he relied. Some of them doubtless, had also a good deal of oral information which had not been reduced to writing. That, then, is the way our present Gospels came into being; they are built upon written manuscripts, the manuscripts themselves being built upon oral teaching.

Soon the Gospels were regarded as so authoritative that, by degrees, they too were read in the synagogue services. Sometimes the Epistles, sometimes these Gospel narratives were read side by side with the Jewish Scriptures, so that at last they took on the same sacred character as was already attributed to the Jewish Scriptures themselves. It is, of course, a long time before we get the fixed canon of the New Testament. But, nevertheless, you already have the beginnings of the canon. The Bible is one of the greatest institutions of the Christian Church. It was so in the beginning as it is to-day, but at that time the Bible was still in the process of formation.

The Buildings

Then, again, one of the interesting elements of the new organization would be the buildings in which Christians worshipped. I imagine that the first place in which they met would be some upper room, such as that in which the Last Supper was held. No doubt, as the numbers multiplied, something more adequate than the upper room would be needed, and it is possible that one of the wealthier Christians who lived in a house constructed after the Roman style would,

did

perhaps, allow the Christians to use a room opening upon the forecourt. Many people have tried to find in the characteristic Roman structure a plan of the original Christian church. Personally I think it is a great mistake; it is a view which most of us abandoned a long time ago. The original plan of the Christian Church is not to be found in the Roman dwelling-house, but in the Jewish synagogue. Even when dwelling-houses were adapted for Christian worship they were adapted very much in the form of the synagogue.

You may ask, What was the characteristic synagogue plan? Well, it was a plain, oblong building. There were seats along the north and the south sides, as we should call them; and there was a raised structure at the 'east' end. There were no seats in the middle; people who were capable of standing were expected to stand; only the aged and infirm were expected to use the seats at the sides. Around what we should call the east end were grouped a row of seats which were occupied by the elders. In the middle of them was a more pretentious seat which was obviously regarded as a sort of throne intended for the president, or presiding elder. This is precisely the picture which is given us in the Book of the Revelation of the worship in Heaven. John, in his vision, describes the elders seated around the throne, but he doubles the number, twenty-four instead of twelve, which was the usual number. You emphasized the importance of a thing if you doubled it, either in number or in size. And because the number of the elders was doubled it did emphasize the importance of the One on the throne to whom reference is made. But this is the interesting fact, that the earliest Christian churches of which we have any knowledge show precisely this same seating arrangement; there is no break from the arrangement of the Jewish synagogue to the arrangement of the Christian Church.

The Ministry

I said a moment ago that nowadays scholars are much more ready to trace the origin of their Christian buildings from the Jewish surroundings than from the Græco-Roman environment. The importance of this comes out quite clearly, when you think of the next institution of the early Christian Church, namely, the ministry. Where does the Christian ministry come from? Some have said it came from the Græco-Roman world, and that the bishop was nothing more or less than the steward of the pagan club. I think there are very few scholars who would accept that conclusion to-day. It seems quite clear that the origin of the ministry is to be found in the Jewish Church. We know how St. Paul sent delegates to appoint elders in certain churches. If you think of the Jewish organization, with its elders, you find precisely that that is what the early Christians accepted for the Christian Church. The elders had their assistants, and those assistants were people whom we should describe as deacons, although it is not certain whether at the beginning the diaconate was an office, or a function. Nevertheless you can see that just as there were deacons, or assistants in the synagogue, so they would naturally appoint similar officers in the Christian Church. Thus you have your elder and your deacon coming straight over from Judaism into the Christian Church. The difficulty, of course, is the Bishop.

He always is the difficulty! And he is the difficult person to place in the early history of the ministry. I think that Dom Gregory Dix and the Bishop of Oxford are right in laying emphasis upon the institution of the Apostolate. Our Lord had His apostles; so had the Great Synagogue its apostles in Jerusalem. It is a well-known institution; they were delegates, plenipotentiaries sent out to do the work of the organization that sent them. And just as the Great Synagogue sent out its apostles to attend to the affairs in some local synagogue, so our Lord sent out His apostles to do the work He wanted to be done. It was they who were expected to carry on the work of the Gospel when He was removed from this earthly scene. They and their delegates would ultimately settle down in those local churches when their work as plenipotentiaries was done. The individual apostle would take over the personal care of one such congregation. And where would he be seated? There was only one possible place, and that would be the seat of the presiding elder. And so you have your local

Bishop. I cannot see why we need go any further to look for the origin of the Bishop. I admit that the evidence is not completely conclusive, but the evidence for the origin of any institution is very seldom entirely conclusive. At the same time there is very little of real vital criticism that can be brought against that particular suggestion. You have your seating arrangement passed over from the Jewish synagogue to the Christian Church; and there must be officers to fit it. If you have that sort of seating arrangement it seems to cry aloud for the Bishop, the apostolic representative, to be seated in that particular seat designed for the president.

The Liturgy

There is just one other institution I must mention, and that is the Liturgy. I mention this because I have a very different idea of the origin of the Eucharist from that which is common to scholars to-day, and if I have a little historical heresy I should like to ventilate it so that you have a chance of rebuking me later on. It is generally assumed that the Eucharist was associated with some full meal. People take it for granted that there was some Agape, or love-feast, and that the Eucharist was something tacked on to this. I revolt very definitely from that common assumption. I do not believe that the Eucharist ever had any association in the beginning with anything like the Agape. I believe the Eucharist was a repetition of the ritual act performed by our Lord Himself in the Upper

Room. He was evidently accustomed to hold a 'fellow-ship meal' with His disciples frequently. He took part in the blessing of bread and wine associated with it on the eve of great occasions, or on the eve of the Sabbath. It was a well-known institution of the synagogue; people who were friends joined together and formed for the occasion what was formally a congregation so that the particular rite might be observed.

But on the night before He suffered Jesus gave this rite an entirely new and unique significance. When He blessed the bread and the wine, He said: 'This is My Body. This is My Blood.' Whatever peculiar meaning you put into those words, it is quite clear that He is starting this particular institution on an entirely new course of development, just as He had started the Church on a new course of development. It is associated with Himself, and I believe our Lord meant to imply that those who partook of the bread and wine would be made sharers in His personality, in His vital energy, in His Body and Blood. That was not a full meal. It was the partaking of a small piece of bread, and the sipping of the chalice of wine. I believe that careful attention to the details in regard to the origin of this institution would tend to make us believe that this was a special rite, and not a full meal.

What about the Agape? Where does that come in? I think it would be very difficult to find any trace of the Agape in the earliest records. Personally I do not believe that the love-feast came in, as far as orthodox circles are concerned, until fairly late, and by fairly late I mean about the close of the second century. You say, What about St. Paul and the Corinthians? Does he not rebuke them because 'in eating every one taketh before other his own supper; and one is hungry, and another is drunken'? Precisely. St. Paul is rebuking them because they did not know the real meaning of the Lord's Supper. What St. Paul is saying is 'You must not have this full meal as your Eucharist. You have got the whole thing wrong. You in Corinth, you want your brighter services, but you cannot get them that way. You cannot have a jollification, and then call that the Lord's Supper. Our service is something entirely different. There were certain things that our Lord did on the night He was betrayed. You must stick closely to what He did; and that is what you call the Lord's Supper.' Is not that the way in which St. Paul is dealing with the question? In other words, to associate the Eucharist with some full meal was a complete aberration. I think that if you examine the case carefully you will see that there is no strong argument in favour of the view that there ever was a time when the Agape, plus the Eucharist, was the normal thing for the true Christian Church.

The Spirit of the Period

That is all I have time to deal with. Let me try to draw my remarks to a conclusion, and to say that in all this I am not trying to give you a chronicle of events, not to deal so much with details, but to bring out what I conceive to be the spirit of the particular age. Here in this period which we have dealt with this afternoon, it seems to me that there are abundant signs of unity and authority. The Christian Church is feeling its own feet, realizing it has been sent by God with a definite task to perform, and having the courage to perform it, even though it is brought into disrepute in certain circles. But more and more, having realized its own authority, and having made its attempt to win the whole nation of the Jews, and having failed in that attempt, the Church is driven back to a realization of the importance of the Christian message for the individual soul. Jesus came to redeem His people from their sins. Christians thought, quite rightly, that that meant the nation as a whole, but when the nation would not accept the message, they were compelled to apply it to the case of the individual soul. And there is the lesson for many of us to-day. We know, we who are clergy, that we are the parsons, the *personae* of God, and of the Church in a particular area. Often we wish to God that we could claim the whole of our district for Christ. But the people we are dealing with are only an infinitesimal fraction of the people living in that area. We are in precisely the same position as were our forebears in the Early Church. When they knew that they could not get the whole community, then, without losing sight of their ultimate aim, they turned to the immediate work of saving the individual. That is what you and I are often forced to do to-day.

C

II

THE CONQUEST OF EMPIRE

AT the close of my last lecture I sought to point out that the period of Church history which had been covered revealed the Church, in the defeat of its attempt to win the Jewish people, falling back upon the effort to bring salvation to individual souls. In the period which I shall hope to cover this afternoon we shall see the Church recapturing its position, and more than recapturing it, actually conquering the Roman Empire.

The Lord's Supper

I should, however, first of all like to refer to one question which has been put to me since our last lecture. It was pointed out that I had spoken of my own belief that there never had been a close association between the Eucharist and any full meal, such as that which is described in the name Agape. I have been asked to explain why in that case the New Testament tells us that our Lord took the cup *after* supper. As a matter of fact St. Luke's account of the Last Supper records the use of two cups. The precise position and relation of what we call the chalice to the ceremony as a whole has given rise to a great deal

of perplexity on the part of scholars, so much perplexity, in fact, that some of them suggest that in the
beginning there was no chalice at all! I do not, I need
hardly say, accept that conclusion.

I think we have to remember that what is in consideration is not a full meal, such as would be suggested
by the Passover ceremony. The idea that the Eucharist
was associated directly with the Passover has been
almost entirely abandoned by scholars. The Eucharist
was not celebrated at the time when the Passover was
being held, but on the evening before. Our Lord
was crucified at the time that the paschal lamb was
slain, consequently the Lord's Supper took place on
the evening before. Although it was not the Passover
itself, it was part of a ceremony which took place in
preparation as I suggested last time, not only for the
Passover, but for every great feast, and very often as
a preliminary to the Sabbath itself. It was the Qiddush,
a blessing with a ceremonial eating of bread and drink-
ing of wine, which was a customary celebration on the
part of a family, or a small body of people, who could
regard themselves as being a synagogue. There is
no doubt, as again I suggested last time, that our Lord
and His disciples were accustomed to mark solemn
occasions by such meals—token meals—solemn ceremonial meals. We know very little about the details.
But there was actually a breaking and eating of bread,
and there was the passing round of several cups of
wine; and in either case there was a blessing, which,
in the characteristic Jewish fashion, was a thanks-

giving to God, rather than an actual consecration of the bread and wine.

It must have been some ceremony of that kind at which our Lord, when He broke the bread, said 'This is My Body,' and when He passed round the chalice in the customary fashion, said, 'This is My Blood.' And the significant thing is that that celebration, apart from any association it may have had with any other sort of meal, or occasion, was repeated over and over again in memory of that which our Lord had done originally. We have, I think, no sufficient evidence that in the subsequent celebrations of this particular ceremony there was actually any association with a full meal. We know that the Qiddush at one stage of its history was separated from the meal and celebrated in the synagogue. In view of the special significance attached to the Bread and Wine by our Lord it is natural to think of the Christian rite as equally separable. That is the point I was trying to emphasize. The suggestion that the chalice which our Lord took 'after Supper' implies actually a full meal need not apply to any subsequent celebrations. In any case I suggest the repetition was never associated by orthodox circles with the Agape until comparatively late in the development of liturgical practice when all danger of confusion was past. That is my own interpretation of what took place, and I am quite prepared to acknowledge that very few scholars would agree with me. But there it is for what it is worth, and I feel it is worthy of consideration.

Persecution

Now to revert to our subject for this afternoon. After it had once become thoroughly launched, and clearly distinct from any other organization in the minds of those who belonged to it, the Church entered straight upon a period of persecution which lasted for three centuries.

Now I am not going to give you picturesque details of life in the catacombs, where, in the popular imagination the Christians sought refuge from their persecutors. As a matter of fact the catacombs were no place in which to hide, because they were all carefully mapped and the documents were kept by the authorities; and everybody knew everything about the catacombs, just as everybody would know about cemeteries to-day. So that there could be no question of that being a secret hiding-place for the Christians. Nevertheless, Christians did worship in the catacombs, partly for convenience sake, and partly because of the association they would have with the dead who were buried there, and partly also because they were out of the gaze of prying eyes. As a result of the work of excavation there has been discovered one staircase which might have provided a bolt-hole for any who wanted to make a quick get-away. But there is no suggestion that the actual place of worship was a secret one.

You might wonder why anybody should wish to persecute a harmless body like the early Christians. The answer is because they were so different from the people in their neighbourhood. They would seem to their neighbours to be rather a joyless kind of people because they would not take part in the ordinary festivals. The reason for that was because the feasts and the festivals were largely connected with pagan sacrifices, and so the Christians could not take part in them. They got the reputation for exhibiting a kind of melancholia which fixed itself in the minds of those with whom they had to do. Consequently when Nero set fire to part of Rome he found it easy to father the suspicion of arson upon the Christians. He made them the scapegoats, and he put them to one of the fiercest persecutions that they had to suffer. Some of them he smeared with pitch, and used as torches to light his gardens; he clothed others of them in the skins or wild beasts, and set dogs upon them.

There are two records of that particular persecution in the New Testament; one in the First Epistle of St. Peter where we seem to be balanced on the knife-edge of a period in which it is uncertain whether that persecution will remain in Rome, or whether it will spread throughout the whole of the Roman Empire. If you read that Letter carefully, you will see that St. Peter urges the Christians to give no ground or suspicion to the Roman soldiers, or police. He says: 'If you have got to suffer, see you suffer for no other cause than your adherence to the Name of Jesus. If you suffer for the Name, glory in it; but do not suffer because of having done something to arouse the suspicion of the mob, or of the police. Be circumspect in your conduct, and in all that you do.' The other record is in the Apocalypse where the original loyalty of the Christians to the Empire has turned to intense hatred of 'the whore of Babylon.'

Having once begun, there was a tendency on the part of the authorities to persecute the Church repeatedly. We are, however, not to suppose that Christians were subject to persecution throughout the whole of the first three centuries of their history. But because they were known as the members of an 'unlicensed religion,' therefore when any trouble arose they were unprotected. If there was a war on things went badly for the Church; the Government would look round for scapegoats, and find them in the Christians. If the Jews wanted to divert dislike from themselves they would direct it to the Christians. If some one had a particular neighbour whom he wished to be rid of, he could always start an outcry against the Christians. From any one of these causes persecution might arise. But, so far as I am aware, there was no universal persecution of Christians until the end of the second century. Then the Emperors began to turn their attention to this underground movement. The authorities realized its strength, and felt they must do something about it; they began to display a certain amount of knowledge of the Christian organization, and they used that knowledge in order to try to destroy the Church as a whole.

One of the most interesting experiments was undertaken by Severus at the beginning of the third century.

He thought his best plan would be to try to attack the Church in its weakest part; not the fully established members, but the catechumens, who were coming forward for baptism, and preparing to enter the Church. He thought if he could cut off the supply of membership at its source, the Church would die. Naturally that kind of persecution was felt most at the great educational centres. In Alexandria, for instance, Origen himself would certainly have suffered if his mother had not carried out the age-old tactics of mothers when they want to keep their boys from going out and hidden his clothes. Origen could not get out, and so was saved from death. It was in that persecution that there suffered St. Perpetua and St. Felicity. Perpetua was a Roman matron, and Felicity was her slave. Felicity had a baby born to her in the prison, and she rejoiced, she said, in passing from the presence of the midwife to the executioner's knife. Perpetua's prison became a palace to her when her own baby was brought to her. The populace saw the matron and her slave suffer death together. That was the finest example of the unity established between the various classes through a common love for our Lord that the pagan world had ever seen.

An experiment of quite a different kind was made by Decius half-way through that century, about A.D. 250. He tried to seize not the catechumens, but the leaders. He believed that, by so doing, he would make the whole organization fall to pieces. He attacked the leaders, particularly the bishops. It put them in a very difficult situation. If they ran away, then they would be accused of cowardice. On the other hand, if they stayed they would certainly be taken and executed, and so the organization would be destroyed. St. Cyprian, one of the greatest of them, faced the opprobrium and fled. He managed to secrete himself first in one place, and then in another, and he administered his diocese as best he could. Later, when he was more confident of the issue, he allowed himself to be taken and was, in due course, martyred.

At the end of the century there came a much more determined persecution inaugurated by Diocletian. That was a concerted effort to attack first one section of the membership, and then another, and to try by all means to get the organization destroyed. It was in that persecution that our own protomartyr, St. Alban, suffered in this country; so far had the persecution spread. It was not spasmodic, but it was carefully organized, and spread throughout the whole of the Roman empire.

I am not sure whether the period of persecution was not, in some respects, the noblest part of our history. Certainly some of the finest characters we have to look back upon were produced during those three centuries. You think of Polycarp examined before the magistrate, and ordered to forswear Christ. 'Eighty and six years have I served Him' he said, 'and He did me no wrong; how can I now deny my King who has saved me?' That is the old man's answer, which he supported with his life. At the other end of the scale you have the boy Tarcisius, whose business it was to take the Reserved Sacrament to the sick, and who, as he carried the Host, was stopped by the sentry and, refusing to give it up, paid the forfeit with his life. You have the girl Blandina who was led through every kind of torture until she was at last despatched. It was that kind of courage, that readiness to witness to the faith with one's life, that set the seal to Christianity, and made people realize it was something which had to be taken seriously.

The persecution came to an end, of course, when the Roman Empire saw that the Church had grown powerful; and that conclusion was reached under the leadership of the man who was crowned Emperor here in England—Constantine. The story is well-known how, before the battle of the Milvian Bridge, he saw in the sky a shining cross, and the words 'In this sign thou shalt conquer.' It was that vision which apparently persuaded him to throw in his lot with the Christians to the extent that he would ensure toleration of their worship. We are naturally inclined to magnify that particular incident, and to think of him as an avowed Christian from that day onward; but I think that is, probably, something of an exaggeration. Constantine was a figure characteristic of his time. He was a statesman, a soldier, and he was determined to try to cement his empire by using this particular force which others had tried to destroy. If Christianity was there to reckon with, why not make it a friend, and use it? That Constantine was prepared to do when he decided to tolerate Christianity, but he thus set free the Church to do the work that it had been preparing all these years to do.

Church and State

But before we discuss that work I would like to spend a few moments in trying to draw out for you the actual relations which existed throughout this period between the Church and the State. I pointed out last time that the Christian Church had its origin in the Jewish Church; and the Jewish Church, you remember, was simply one aspect of a single entity which in another aspect was known as the State. The State and the Church were simply two sides of the same shield. You might have thought that that kind of thing would have passed over into Christianity; and so it might have done. But, as we have seen, Christianity failed to convert the whole of the Jewish nation; and for a time, the Christian Church was hidden, so to speak, under the shield of Judaism. The Romans were, on the whole, a very tolerant and politic people; and they did give recognition to the Jewish religion. They saw that the Jews were a peculiar people, who had no images, or visible representation of their God; they knew that they had peculiar customs; they knew they were a very stubborn people. And rather than knock their heads against a brick wall, they said, Very well, we recognize you; you can be a licensed religion; you can practise your own particular religion without let or hindrance.

For a time, they did not recognize the difference between the Christians and the Jews. Claudius, we know, drove the Jews and the Christians together out of Rome because of some dispute that had arisen—'under the instigation of Christ' which was the nearest that the contemporary historian could get to a realization of what the trouble was about. Obviously there had been some disturbance between the Jews residing in the ghetto and the Christians. But later the Emperors did recognize the difference. As we have seen, Nero took the opportunity of that difference to make the Christians the scapegoats for his burning of Rome.

From the period of Nero something very definite happened to the relationship between the Church and the State. It is usually assumed that from the time of Nero the Christians were completely banned; that is why it is supposed they were always subject to persecution. But they were only occasionally subject to persecution by reason of the fact that while some emperors were prepared to ignore them, others were determined to persecute them very bitterly. The difficulty was that they were reckoned as an unlicensed religion, and that being so, they had to stand against all sorts of attacks if any trouble arose from any reason whatsoever. That seems to me to be the most likely interpretation of events. That is why during the next two and a half centuries you get alternations between comparative peace for the Christians, and persecution.

That does not mean that the Christians were entirely free from the State in the administration of their own affairs. I want to emphasize this point, because one sometimes hears one's colleagues say how nice it would be if the Church could be free of all State connection, thinking it is possible to be in such a condition. But the Church can never be entirely free from the State. The Christians found that in the Roman Empire. On one occasion an interesting situation arose when a certain amount of property, which had been claimed by a heretical teacher, was, as a matter of fact, adjudicated to the Church by a pagan Government. Aurelian, in adjudicating that property to the Church, had to lay down certain definitions of the doctrinal position. The people whom he allowed to take charge of the property were to be those who held the same doctrine as the Bishops in Rome and in Italy; that is to say, his own particular neighbourhood. Thus a pagan State has to decide on a question of church doctrine before it can perform its proper function and deal with a dispute over property. You can never be entirely free of the State.

Of course, a very different attitude was adopted by the State under Constantine. Although, as I have just said, it would be a mistake to regard Constantine from the time of the battle of the Milvian Bridge as a complete and earnest Christian, nevertheless he did institute the toleration of Christians, and that in a formal manner. The normal way of putting this is to say that in A.D. 313 he issued an 'Edict of Milan,' which many people think actually 'established' the Christian Church—a very gross perversion of history. For one thing nobody has yet been able to discover the Edict of Milan; although you find it mentioned in all the history books, no one knows where it is. Actually what did happen was that Constantine and Licinius agreed together that under their united regime they would tolerate all religions, Christianity among them. Probably some sort of codicil was agreed allowing for a universal toleration of religion. This, of course, permitted the Christian Church henceforth to go on its way unmolested. What it did was to put the Christian Church on an equality with the other religions. Later in his reign Constantine begins to raise the Christian Church to a higher level than the pagan sects. A great deal of the more humane legislation which was introduced at this time can, I think, be attributed directly to the influence of Christianity. I am not saying that Constantine was an ideal person. He was not, certainly not to the members of his own family whom he did away with. But you do find from this time onward, for instance, that debtors are no longer to be branded on the face; that slaves who are moved from one place to another are no longer to be separated from their families, but are to be permitted to go into their bondage together; and even the post-horses are no longer to be ill-treated. It is that kind of humane legislation which does suggest a change in the temper of the time, and shows how Christian influence has begun to make itself felt.

It was not under Constantine that the Church was established; that was done under Theodosius in 380. Theodosius published an Edict establishing the Church; and he gave a definition as to what the Catholic Church was. There are others who put their own interpretation on the term Catholic. But Theodosius said that he would regard those people as Catholics and would allow those people to use the name of Catholic, who were in communion with the Bishops of Rome and Alexandria, and who held a belief in the Trinity in Unity. Those were the terms under which he established the Christian Church in the Roman Empire.

Doctrinal Definition

Having thus seen the Church established, let us go back over the period again, and look at it from another point of view. One of the interesting features of the period is the gradual definition of Christian doctrine, and that definition begins almost at once. You find one doctrinal system being built up by St. Paul; but you get a very different approach under a writer like St. John; and I would suggest that you get a sort of 'central' approach from St. Peter in his First Epistle, and, possibly, in the synoptic Gospels as well. But these systems were not complete systems; they were the seed plots of future systems. People inevitably began to argue about the various aspects of Christian doctrine; they desired to delve more deeply into it, and to define it more clearly. And in the effort to define Christian doctrine, people's characters were revealed. Sometimes the definition shows only too clearly that what they are trying to do is to get rid of those parts which seem to them to be hard and difficult. I think the most conspicuous case was that of the Gnostics; they longed for esoteric knowledge; what they wanted was a Christianity without tears, a thing which is impossible, of course. They wanted to get rid of the offence of the Cross, and make it unnecessary for people to feel they must go through the process of being crucified to the world, or allowing the world to be crucified to them. They tried, in a sort of pseudo-scientific way, to change the hard core of Christian doctrine into a kind of Christian philosophy. One of their favourite ideas was that instead of there being an Incarnation of the Eternal Word in human nature, there was a process by which the spiritual became mixed up with the material. If you can imagine the atmosphere condensing into moisture, and then the moisture hardening into ice, you get some sort of idea of the way in which, according to the Gnostics, the spiritual became embodied in the material. Salvation was gained by setting the spiritual free, but that end was reached by almost any means but the suffering of the Cross. The Theosophists are the nearest modern parallel to the Gnostics.

Another interesting effort to carry Christian doctrine a stage further, and one which, I think, was in some ways much more laudable, was that of the Montanists who, in their effort to stand up to persecution, produced a certain kind of fanaticism; they believed themselves to be inspired, and took the most extreme steps on every occasion. Among other things they found the world in which they lived so very degenerate a place that they decided to get away from it altogether, and they started to prepare for the new Jerusalem in the wilds of Asia Minor. They also believed that they had been granted a new incarnation of the Holy Spirit which was comparable to the Incarnate Word in Jesus of Nazareth. They believed they were so animated by the Spirit that they could actually produce a new revelation which would supersede the old revelation which had been given by Jesus of Nazareth.

These are examples of the way in which people tried to define the Christian doctrine beyond that which was given in the foundation documents and in the memory of those who came into contact with our Lord as His disciples. As to the means by which the Christian Church tried to stop this deterioration of its doctrine, it had, first of all, the Scriptures; and it began to define the canon of Scripture so that it could say precisely which books were to be regarded as sacred, and which not. The process was a long one, but the collection was gradually solidified into a corpus of sacred books. By this means it became possible to say precisely what proof texts could be relied upon, and what could not be relied upon.

Another means by which the leaders held the Church together, and prevented the spread of false teaching, was, of course, the ministry. The important fact about

D

the ministry was its claim to apostolic succession. 'If you really want to know what the apostolic teaching is, it is no good going to the Gnostics. You can tell at once if you go to the churches which have an apostolic succession, which bishop can trace his doctrine back to the apostles themselves.' That is the argument of Irenaeus. The succession of the Bishops from the apostles was fundamental as guaranteeing the correctness of the doctrinal position.

Then the third way in which the leaders could protect the Christian doctrine against the influence of the heretic was by the development of the creed. The creed originally came into use in connection with baptism. Possibly it was no more in the first beginnings than a declaration that 'Jesus is Lord'; and candidates could not be baptized until they were prepared to make that declaration. Side by side with this, or, perhaps, a little later, there was the custom of asking the catechumen at his baptism whether he believed, not simply in Jesus as Lord, but whether he believed in the Trinity. The concluding verses of St. Matthew's Gospel seem to suggest that that custom came in almost at once. And soon the Bishop, in his own particular community, would base his teaching on the three-fold answer. He would explain to the catechumens what is meant by saying they believed in God the Father, God the Son, and God the Holy Spirit. And he would include, too, his own explanations of the main facts and details upon which the Christian doctrine was built. It was in that way that the

Apostles' Creed was originally developed; it was the baptismal creed.

When Constantine gave toleration to the Christian Church, which brought about a tremendous expansion of Christian life in every way, then, of course, a great effort was made to find a still fuller, and more satisfactory expansion and development of the Christian creed, which would meet new difficulties that had arisen. By this time the Church was fully launched into the stream of Græco-Roman civilization, and it had to explain itself in the light, not merely of Roman law, but also of Greek philosophy; and the ordinary, plain, everyday creed which simply said what God had done was no longer satisfactory, because the Greeks thought about God and religion in a different way from that which was characteristic of the Hebrews. In the Old Testament the main point about God is that He is the Creator, the God who acts; the Greek was not so much concerned about what God does, as about what God is. That led on to a tremendous expansion of the creed. If you compare the Apostles' Creed with the Nicene Creed, and read them carefully together, you will see how different they are in their attitude towards the whole subject. The Apostles' Creed is quite content to give the historical facts; the Nicene Creed wants to give philosophical explanations of the Nature of God and the Person of Christ.

The effort to solve this particular problem in the period beginning with Constantine led to the calling together of a vast number of Ecclesiastical Councils.

There were various points which agitated them, mostly concerned with the relation between the divine and the human in Christ. That was supremely important in the realm of psychology as well as in the realm of theology, because it did lead people to delve very deeply into the question of personality. I think that we can regard it, in the divine providence, as being a very valuable thing that these questions should have been so carefully examined at this period.

I, personally, cannot help feeling sorry for some of those, who, in their anxiety to probe to the bottom of the truth overstepped the line of orthodoxy. I feel particularly sorry for Apollinarius, who, though a heretic, does deserve our compassion. He was trying to find out exactly how the Eternal Word could co-operate with human nature so as to make only one Personality. If, he argued, when the human Jesus joined with the Eternal Word, you got only one Person, then the Eternal Word must have replaced the human soul in Jesus; and what you had was really a human body combined with a divine soul. That view was so obviously wrong that I cannot think that Apollinarius put it forward seriously. He must have been in the early stage of his thinking about these things. Later, instead of thus splitting the personality into two, he learnt to distinguish three elements—the soul, the spirit, the body. He was then dealing with the problem in a much more scholarly way. What he said then was that the *Logos* must have replaced the spirit in Jesus of Nazareth, so that the personality of Jesus consisted of a human body, a human soul, and the divine spirit. That does deserve looking at very carefully, but I am quite sure that the Church was fully right in rejecting it. What the Church said was: 'If the Eternal *Logos*, the Word of God, did not assume the human spirit, then He could not have redeemed the human spirit. What He did not assume He could not redeem. Consequently, we cannot agree that there is anything less than the totality of human nature in the Incarnate Jesus of Nazareth. He must have assumed the totality of human nature, or the totality of human nature cannot be redeemed.' Finally, as you know, the Church came to the conclusion that there was in Jesus of Nazareth a human body, a human soul, and a human spirit; that which was peculiar, so to speak, to the Eternal *Logos* was just that last ultimate element which implies personality and individuality, which distinguishes one person from another. But it was with the whole of human nature— body, soul, and spirit—that the Eternal Word identified Himself. That was the conclusion to which the Church came after very much argumentation.

Growing Elaboration

We cannot help realizing that we are now in a very different atmosphere from that in which we began this lecture. The Church had then just emerged as a separate entity; we have reached now the position where the Church is established in the Roman Empire; where it has conquered the civilized world; where it can actually, on occasions, almost dictate to the governments of the world; where the emperor Constantine is proud to call himself 'the Bishop of those without.' It shows that he did not think it entirely out of keeping to suggest that he might occupy a sort of authoritative position within the Christian Church. How different from the attitude of Nero, when the Church was only an underground movement.

Nowhere is this change more clearly seen than in the growing elaboration of worship. The humble service of the Upper Room and the Catacombs is now beautified and ennobled by every known art. Not only in worship is this different attitude to be marked, but in the buildings where that worship is conducted. In Jerusalem, in Rome, in Constantinople, the Emperor himself is building churches. In place of the crudely painted symbols of the fish, representing Christ, and the butterfly representing the soul, there are now brilliant mosaics, the fruit of the most up-to-date art of the period. And the churches themselves are no longer tiny imitations of the Jewish synagogue, but are built after the fashion of the Roman town halls; they are splendid both in their exterior, and in their interior. The organization of the Church has also become much more elaborate. You no longer have a bishop, with, perhaps, a personal attendant and a few elders assisting him, but you have a place like Rome divided into seven archdeaconaries, with a total of a hundred and fifty attendant ministers. In other words, the Church was becoming something which, though naturally associated with the stable at Bethlehem, is now more easily associated with the courts of kings. Put that side by side with the change that has come in the creeds, and in the general interpretation of Christian doctrine, and you realize how greatly the position of the Church has changed.

Dr. Inge goes so far as to say that after Constantine there was not much that was good. I must say, I think that is a very exaggerated statement. I think of people like Athanasius, Ambrose, Martin—those lovely characters. I know that there is room for people to deprecate some of the changes that took place. The characters of many of the Christians were not so fine as those who lived during the period of persecution. Even Walter Hilton can say with regard to them that Peter's net became so full of fish it was well-nigh breaking. Nevertheless, I am bound to say that, in my view, looking at it as dispassionately as I can, there is no authority whatever for saying either that the faith has changed its essential character, or that the Church has changed from being what it was to something else. What has happened is that the Church has developed from a defeated organization which could not convert its own nation, and had to concentrate on the conversion of the individual, to a Church which has converted the world empire, and which is able to influence public opinion, and ministers, not merely to the individual, but to the whole of society. And where you have such a change of opportunity, then you must adapt yourself to it. I believe that the change

that you can see in the post-Constantine Church is
attributable simply to that fact. Although there comes
in a great deal of abuse, yet, nevertheless, in spite of
those abuses, the Church has an opportunity of doing
the work to which it had been called in far greater
measure than it was ever able to do it before. It has
fought its fight; it has won its battle. Now it sits on
the throne of kings. It cannot shrink from exercising
the influence of kings.

III

THE CONQUEST OF BARBARISM

IN our second Lecture we discussed the history of
the Christian Church between the end of the first
and the end of the fourth century. We noticed how
the Church overcame the resistance of the whole
Roman Empire, and to such effect that it actually
became the established religion within the Empire.

I was rather surprised that during the week's interval
since my last Lecture no one has written to point out
to me that in that Lecture covering three centuries
I failed to discuss the great Councils of the period.
Well, perhaps some of you were much relieved that I
did not introduce you to the morass of intellectual dis-
cussions about the theological niceties that formed the
main considerations of those Councils. But perhaps
I ought, for the sake of completeness, to say that as a
matter of fact there were four universal or Oecumenical
Councils. At the meeting of the Council of Nicæa the
Church decided that our Lord was perfect God. In
the Council of Constantinople it decided that He was
perfect Man. In the third great Council at Ephesus it
decided that our Lord was one Person. And in the
last great Council at Chalcedon it decided that He
had two natures. So that the great fundamental

doctrines about the Person of our Lord were established at that period.

Barbarian Invasions

But now to address ourselves to the task that faces us this afternoon. We have to try to cover a period which is generally known as that of the Dark Ages, or as some historians call it, the Early Middle Ages. We shall see here that the Church, having first conquered the great Roman Empire, now has a fresh task to accomplish. It has to overcome the hordes of barbarians who, in fact, broke up that Empire. And we shall see that, in order to do that, it has to make a definite effort to baptize the contemporary culture into the name and the faith of Christ.

First, let us try to get an over-all picture of the break-up of the Roman Empire. You realize, of course, the essential weakness of the situation of the Empire. The frontier was enormous, and far too great for the Roman legions to hold permanently. The first intensive pressure came from the north, when the Goths began to infiltrate towards the Danube. They came originally from some Scandinavian country to the Baltic where they divided into two parts: Ostrogoths to the East, and Visigoths to the West. They began to press further down until they came upon the outlying fringes of the Roman Empire, and presently they began to break the line of the Danube, and to make inroads across it into the firmly established part of the Empire. The first great catastrophe came when

Decius met them in 253, and was defeated and killed, 'the first Roman Emperor to die fighting against a foreign foe on Roman soil.' That was a disaster indeed, but worse was to follow. After a time there came many efforts to press the Goths back behind the line of the Danube until 378, when the Emperor Valens, too impatient to await the arrival of assisting forces from the West, attacked the enemy, and was defeated and slain in a great battle at Adrianople. That was one of the epoch-making battles of the world because it affected military tactics to a great extent. The Roman infantry had hitherto been found invincible in the long run. But now the fleet-footed Goths had been able to overcome the heavy armed Romans. The latter for the first time lost faith in their infantry, and began to rely much more on cavalry.

However, the change did not avail to save the very heart and centre of the Empire. In the year 410 Rome was attacked, and fell before the Goths under Alaric. The thrill of horror that passed through the whole of the civilized world at that news is reflected in the great work of St. Augustine, *The City of God*. One can realize something of the sensation that would be caused by this rapid break-up of a power which had ruled the whole of the civilized world for so many centuries.

When the Goths themselves began to be pressed upon by fresh hordes of barbarians coming down from the central Russian steppes it looked as if once again Rome would fall. But in this particular instance it was saved by the Church. The fact that the centre of

government had been removed from Rome had left
the Bishop in supreme command of the situation, and
he was looked upon by the whole population, and not
merely by the Church people, as their natural saviour.
And when Attila came with his Huns, Pope Leo, with
a couple of members of the senate, went out to meet
him (the meeting has been portrayed in well-known
pictures). Whatever may be the precise details of what
took place at that time, it is a fact that the Pope over-
awed the Hun leader to such an extent that he persuaded him to retreat from Rome and to leave the city
untouched. But it was not spared for very long, for
in 452 a fresh party of barbarians pressed down on
all sides; and the Vandals, under their leader Gaiseric,
attacked Rome, and plundered it in 455.

The question arose: Whose fault was it that the
Empire was being destroyed, and that Rome had been
successfully besieged on so many occasions? The
answer sometimes given was that it was the fault of
Christianity; that the people had forsaken the service of
the old gods, and the gods, being displeased, had
allowed the Empire to fall on these evil days.
Augustine wrote his *City of God* in order to disprove
that argument. He pointed out that in the old days
Rome had suffered many misfortunes but its gods had
been powerless to protect it at that time. Not only so,
but he points out that actually when the first attack
was made upon Rome the very pagans were glad to
take refuge in the Christian Churches, and that the
Gothic leader was himself a Christian of a kind, an

Arian Christian; so he did spare Rome much more than any pagan would have done. And Augustine makes it clear that, so far from Christianity being the cause for the Fall of Rome, it was really the results of paganism which had been responsible for that Fall.

Looking back from this vantage point of time we can see some other reasons why the Empire began to fall to pieces. One of the most important is the growth of nationalism. Precisely the same thing as is happening in the British Commonwealth to-day happened at this period in the Roman Empire. Just as we have a growing nationalism in Eire, in India, in Burma, and in various parts of our Commonwealth, so Rome had to face the growth of nationalism in the various outlying parts of the Empire. Egypt, Persia, Armenia —they all began to feel themselves as separate entities. What they did was to set up rival theologies against that of the Council of Chalcedon, the last of the four great Councils. As a matter of fact these outlying sections of the empire used theology as an excuse for resisting the power of the Emperor in Constantinople. As a result, they did separate themselves, and were thus left open to attack. The worst feature of that was not seen until the seventh century when there came the rise of Islam under the prophet Mahomet. Islam then made rapid progress, because the Roman Empire was no longer bound together by a similarity of Christian doctrine, and a common ideology, and so its border states fell an easy prey to the Mohammedan armies.

Missions

What we want to ask now is: What precisely did the Church do in face of the barbarian invasion? I have already shown how Pope Leo, the acting constitutional head of the municipality, could, by his dominant personality, and did defend Rome against the barbarians. But that in itself was obviously not enough, and the Church realized that it was not enough. From the very early days of the Gothic pressure the Church had begun to do what it could to evangelize the barbarians. One of the greatest names in this connection is that of Ulfilas, an Arian Bishop, one who was prepared to give up the advantages of his own life, and to go across the Danube to evangelize the Goths. He recognized it was not only necessary to preach the Gospel to them, but to reform their whole culture in order that there might be found among them the right kind of environment in which Christian character could be developed. He therefore proceeded first of all to invent a Gothic script for them, thus enabling them to put their ideas into a written language. And having done that, he proceeded to translate for them the Scriptures—not the whole of the Scriptures. He said it was no use translating for them the Books of the Kings because the Goths knew quite enough already about fighting! He sought, nevertheless, to adapt the Christian message in a way in which they were most likely to receive it.

Just as Ulfilas did this work among the Goths, so

other evangelists did it in other outlying parts of the Empire. The part, of course, which interests us, is our own country, and our history in that particular respect is of absorbing interest. When Christianity first came here no one quite knows. If you put aside such legends, for instance, as that about Joseph of Arimathea, and try to get down to the facts, we are reduced to this position. We know that Irenaeus, writing about A.D. 180, omits Britain from the places then reached by the Gospel. But we know also that some time after the turn of the second century Tertullian writing about 208, and Origen writing a little later, both mention Britain as a place to which the Gospel had spread. Obviously, then, the evangelization of Britain took place between those two dates, that is to say, around the end of the second century and the beginning of the third.

The interesting thing is that we have no knowledge of any individual apostle coming to this country, no great evangelist, no hero of the Christian faith, whose name has been written upon the scroll of fame. We are to understand that the people of this country were converted by the rank and file of Christian people who brought Christianity with them as they pursued their ordinary calling. Christianity came in the train of the soldiers and the merchants who travelled to Britain from Gaul. It was thus the ordinary, everyday person who proclaimed the Gospel through his everyday life, and so converted this country to Christ.

We know that presently in the British towns there

were set up a series of dioceses, because we have information that at the Council of Arles in 314 three British Bishops were present. I am the proud successor of one of the Bishops who was present at the Council of Arles—Restitutus, Bishop of London. We know too that the Bishop of York was there; and probably also the Bishop of Lincoln. What happened between A.D. 314 and the end of the sixth century is not very clear. We know that when the Saxons began to come into this country they drove the more efficient of the Britons to the west, but, obviously, a certain number must have remained; you cannot drive a whole people out of a country. Those who remained here seem to have lost their Christianity, and were submerged in the tide of barbarism. But the others found their refuge in Wales, and in Cornwall, and in Cumberland. They were not isolated, because Ireland, for instance, was evangelized by St. Patrick who himself was the son of a British deacon, and had also associations with the Christianity of the Continent. The interesting thing is that it was from Ireland that Christianity crossed back again into England after the Saxon invasion. St. Columba with his companions set up and established a monastery on the island of Iona. From that island was sent St. Aidan to evangelize the English in the north. The British who had been driven into Wales had done nothing in the way of evangelism, because no doubt they found it extremely difficult to contemplate any work of that kind among people who had driven them out of their homes. Nevertheless, a good work was done by Celtic influence in the north, and St. Aidan's is still a name to conjure with in the north of England.

In the year that St. Columba died there landed another mission in the south of England, a mission sent by Pope Gregory; and that mission under St. Augustine began to evangelize the southern part of England. It has been one of the subjects most discussed among Church historians to which of these two missions the main evangelization of England is really due. Well, years ago I had to go into the question rather carefully, and I came to the conclusion that it was just about fifty-fifty. In trying to examine the question without prejudice I could not honestly say that one had done more of the work than the other; it was equally divided. But although the work was evenly distributed between the Celtic mission in the north, and the Italian mission in the south, ultimately I think it was for the good of the Church and for England that the Roman influence became paramount.

The question which of the two types of Christianity England should follow was settled in the Council of Whitby in 664. It was undoubtedly valuable for the future history of the country that England did at that time decide to throw in its lot with the religion of the Continent rather than with the religion of the comparatively small and unknown island of the west. That was, of course, an epoch-making decision, and very soon we derived benefit from it. When Theodore came

E

over to this country, bringing with him, not merely an Italian, but also a Greek strain into the curious stream which went to make up the Christianity of England, he with the enthusiasm of the Eastern, and the administrative ability of the Western, did manage to lay out the whole organization of the Church in this country in a way which would have been quite impossible if we had been left to the rather haphazard zeal of the Celts. Theodore was able to establish a parochial system in a large part of this country. We need not suppose that that was entirely original. I think he took over some conditions which had been found already in paganism. Certainly the parish priests of those days inherited a good many of the functions hitherto performed by the pagan priests. Many of them, for instance, kept the parish bull and boar for breeding purposes. We are always finding fresh jobs for the clergy; I have not yet found that that particular proposal has been started again!

Monasticism

Now I have been talking about the missions to the barbarians, but I have not, so far, mentioned one of the most important instruments that was used for this particular purpose. I suppose, under God, apart from the wonderful work done by certain great individuals, the finest missionary work was done by the monks. Monasticism was very largely responsible for the maintenance of a Christian culture in the Dark Ages. The origin of monasticism itself lies in the mists of antiquity. We do not know where precisely it came from. There are instances of asceticism in some of the pagan religions. Among Christians we know there were individual ascetics who lived a kind of celibate life in their own homes, or sometimes retired for purposes of greater privacy to huts at the foot of their gardens. The first time that Christian monasticism actually appears on the pages of history is when people began to leave their own homes, and go out to live as hermits in the desert. That occurred in Egypt, in the first place, and then, to some extent, in Palestine at the beginning of the fourth century.

The hermits of Egypt were renowned for their great austerity, and for their great zeal. They followed different types, and sometimes it is not easy for us to appreciate the particular type of austerity represented. What we have to realize is that what appeals to the people of one age need not necessarily appeal to people of another. The figure of Simon Stylites standing on top of his pillar seems to us to-day to be rather revolting. But the people of his age who came to listen to him, and saw him there, were made to realize that here was something which they themselves could not possibly emulate, a man who on account of his sheer religious zeal would put himself to this amazing torture. They saw in this austerity a kind of asceticism of the soul, and they were moved by it. We are told that in Syria thousands of people were actually converted as a result of thus coming into contact with him there.

But the hermit life soon began to give place to a more communal type. There was a stage in which the hermits began to gather together for common worship. They lived not very far from each other in cells hollowed out of the rocks, or in huts erected around a sort of open space. The Greek word for open space was lavra, and from that word was derived the title given to this particular stage in monastic life— a kind of half-way house in monasticism, where the old hermit quality still lingers, but where the quality of the true communal life has not yet appeared. Anthony was the leader; he was followed by Ammonius who soon had six hundred disciples in the Nitrian desert.

The third stage was the development of the full common life where people lived together under one roof, sharing their meals and their worship. Pachomius, who had had a military training was the organizer of this type. We find an approach to it even in Caesarea where St. Basil had a considerable number of monks living this kind of life and looking after all sorts of institutions for the young, for the sick, and for the aged. That was the nearest approach to the later development of the monastic life that we get anywhere in the east.

But monasticism, as we know it to-day, really came into this country following the type of St. Benedict, who, in the sixth century issued what he called his 'Little Rule for Beginners.' There he tried to ensure a life which would give people the opportunity of privacy with God, and occasions for carrying out the development of their own characters, and the making of their own souls, and, at the same time, allowing for such variety of work, prayer and study that they would never grow stale in the effort. The regular repetition of the Choir Office was the essential thing, not the saying of Mass, in the Benedictine rule. And side by side with that there was to be allowed time and opportunity for study, and time for manual labour in the gardens, and fields, and elsewhere. The people who followed that kind of rule established houses for themselves in various parts of Europe, and as the barbarian invasion spread, their work became more and more important for their neighbours. There were established everywhere these centres of monastic life, and they became centres, not merely of evangelism, but of education where the old Græco-Roman culture could be handed on to the barbarians impregnated with Christianity, and where they could learn the various arts, and such of the sciences as were available at that time, and also take part in the manual labour carried out in these schools of agriculture and husbandry.

There was still another type of monasticism, and that was the kind to be found in Ireland. In that country they seem to have built up their monasticism along the line of the tribes according to which the whole of society was organized. Nobody, I think, can understand the precise arrangements of these monastic tribes. But the head of the tribe seems to have also conducted as abbot the work of the monastic institution. We know that as the Church in Ireland was developed on those tribal lines, there was no proper diocese, and no diocesan bishop. There were bishops, but they were kept, so to speak, in the tribe, under the rule of the abbot, and they seem to have had no special function apart from ministering certain rites which were kept for the bishop alone, mainly that of ordination.

Northern Europe

The influence of the Church of Ireland upon the Church in this country was very great. Although England had thrown in its lot with continental Christianity, nevertheless those who were the leaders in this country very often had considerable experience of the method of life in Ireland; and the combination of the two resulted in a work of the most tremendous importance for the future history of Europe; because it was from this country that the missionaries went and actually founded the Church and Christian civilization in Northern Europe. The two great names that stand out are those of Willibrord and Boniface; they had both been in Ireland, and had gained some experience there. Willibrord was the bearer of the Gospel to the Frisians and ultimately became Archbishop of Utrecht, while Boniface became Archbishop of Mainz.

They covered an important part of Europe between them. Their lives are extremely fascinating to read. You will find them dealt with in a very brilliant book published last year by Dr. Levison called *England and the Continent in the Eighth Century*. Both of them displayed the same heroic character. They would beard the lion in his den; they would face the barbarians and challenge them. It is a well-known story that Boniface cut down the sacred Oak of Tor, and not only did he do that, but he actually used the planks to make a Mission Chapel. There could have been no more graphic illustration to the barbarians of the powerlessness of their gods, and of the superiority of the Christian God. Another point to notice. Both these men were important because they came to the Continent not only with all this English feeling behind them, but they had the Celtic influence too. Not only so, but when they were on the Continent they were very careful to get into contact with the ruling power at Rome, and to ensure that whatever they did would have the backing of the Roman Church. Consequently, by using the whole of the Christian influence available for them, they were able to stand securely, and to ensure that there should be a proper backing for the Church they were founding. As a result, there was built up on the Continent of Europe a splendid type of Christian life. The English influence was to be seen at its best when the school at York was able to send Alcuin to the court of Charlemagne. At last when Charlemagne was crowned as the holy Roman Emperor in the year 800, then there was seen the consummation of the whole of this tremendous effort to build up a new Christian civilization.

The Change of Culture

It only remains for me to say a word or two about this Christian civilization that was built up. You realize what has happened. The Church is the only institution that survived out of the wreck of the Roman Empire. All other institutions disappeared; the Church survived. The Church was able to take the best elements of the Græco-Roman cultures and impart them to the barbarians. In the monasteries, and in connection with the great cathedrals, there were schools where boys were taught. Here and there you get the teacher who would gather people around him, and who would carry them beyond the limits of primary education. It was the classical education that was given to them; they followed roughly the old lines of education. The simpler subjects were grammar, rhetoric, and dialectics; and the more advanced were arithmetic, geography, astronomy, and music— the famous trivium with the quadrivium imposed upon it.

You can see again the combination of the old Græco-Roman culture with the barbarian strength in the church buildings that began to appear at this time. In them was developed that type of architecture which we know to-day as Norman, and which we should more properly call Romanesque. Here you have the Roman Town Hall, which was the big public building of the early period, showing its influence upon the Christian edifices and the Church using that influence for its own purposes. The new Christian Churches are built very largely on the basilican lines, with the great columns, and the small windows that come from Italy and Southern Europe. They are massive buildings; they have got plenty of room to spread out, and so they cover quite large sites. Their strength lies in their walls, walls that can easily be turned into fortresses, if occasion requires. Here and there a chapel is added in order to provide room for a fresh altar or two. Presently those extra chapels are attached to either side of the long, oblong building, until the whole plan forms that of a cross. There you have the type of building which was common in the early Middle Ages, of which many specimens still remain in this country, and still more on the Continent of Europe.

In the same way you find that the whole social and economic structure begins to develop under the influence of the Christian Church. During the change over a great deal of the land has been taken away from the old Roman owners. Some parts were appropriated by the leaders while others were given to their followers. Presently these leaders began to fall out with each other; and the followers began to huddle round their own particular lord in order to get protection against the attacks of some neighbouring chief. The lord gives his protection to those who seek for it on condition that they render certain kinds of service. So you get on one side the lord protecting his followers, and on their side, the obligation of service in return. There you get the beginning of feudalism, and that feudal system was accepted and used by the Church because there was something essentially Christian that could be worked into it. The idea of the strong protecting the weak is a valuable ideal from the Christian point of view; so also is the idea of mutual service. The Church was able to take this growing system, and to give it its blessing, and to infuse into it that spirit of charity which was a fundamental Christian virtue. Thus in the economical and social development as well as in other departments you see how the Church uses the opportunity to mould the transitional system, impregnating it all the time with the Spirit of Christ. So the Church displays for the first time in history a Christian civilization, the civilization which to-day we still know as European.

Conclusion

That, really, is all I want to say this afternoon. I would like, however, to point out before I end how interesting is the position. We have seen the Church, first of all, failing to convert the Jewish people, and then turning to the salvation of the individual. We have seen next the Church once again having the opportunity to express itself, and to influence, not merely one nation, but the whole civilized world. And in order to do that we saw how it must come out from its primitive condition. From being a sort of underground movement it had to put on the clothing of magnificence; it had to appear in all its grandeur, because, otherwise, it could not have dealt with the nations of the world. It was because of that that Pope Leo could face Attila, and so overawe him that he retreated from Rome. To-day we have come a stage further, and we have realized that, in order to build up the Christian life in man the Church must not merely appeal to the individual or to the Government, but it must see that the environment into which the individual is introduced is such as will enable his character to grow and develop along Christian lines. In other words, the Church, in order to do its work properly, must not only appeal to the individual, it must not only deal with governments, but it must also impregnate the whole of the nation's culture and civilization with the Christian spirit. If in our first lecture we saw the salvation of the individual and in our second the salvation of the Empire, to-day we have seen the salvation of culture.

IV

AUTHORITY *VERSUS* FREEDOM

I BEGAN this Course of Lectures by trying to trace the effort of the Church to ensure the salvation of the individual. In the next period we saw that the main effort of the Church was to ensure the salvation of the nation, or empire. Then in last week's lecture we saw the effort made by the Church to secure the salvation of culture. To-day we have to think about the salvation of freedom.

Pastoral Care

Let us begin by getting the picture as clear as possible in our minds. When the civilized world had settled down after the barbarian invasions, then the Church very rapidly secured a stable organization of its own; and the greater part of Europe, and particularly this country, was divided up into parishes, where was placed one incumbent—leaving out reference to all other clerical help—whose responsibility it was to care for the souls within that particular area. The theory behind this arrangement was that the Church was carrying on our Lord's own work of mediating to mankind the eternal friendship of God; and that task centred in one individual whose official duty it was

to minister to all God's children within his own area.
It was his duty to do there what the whole Church,
both clerical and lay, was expected to do for all
mankind, namely, to mediate to each individual the
love of God.

There was, however, one blot to spoil the harmony
of the whole ideal, and that was the fact that very
early in the medieval period there came a split in the
Church itself. East and West had been growing farther
and farther apart for a considerable time; and not
infrequently they found themselves out of communion with each other. But in the eleventh century
there occurred an unfortunate moment when there
was an intransigent Pope in Rome, and an equally intransigent Archbishop in Constantinople, and the two
were more or less determined if they could not get
their own way, to cause a definite split. At a period
when they had each begun closing the churches and
chapels of the other's nationals in their own area,
they managed to make a reason for excommunicating
each other. Leo IX, in 1054, sent his emissaries to
Constantinople, who placed a bull of excommunication
upon the altar. It is from that date that we reckon the
definitive split between the East and the West. The
theological arguments put up to justify that schism
are of no particular importance. The split was due to
political, and, especially, to personal conditions, and
theology really had little to do with it. But there the
break was caused, which has lasted ever since, and
the breach has never yet been healed.

We, in this lecture, shall have to leave entirely on one side the Eastern half of Christendom, and confine our attention to the Western half, to which we ourselves more particularly belong. In the Western half we have this picture of an area divided into separate districts in each of which one person is placed to be the *persona*, the parson, the official representative of God and His Church, to mediate God's friendship to His people. Now that in itself was a very marked advance in pastoral care, but it was not in itself sufficient to meet the whole need; and soon other means were used to reinforce the pastoral care that was established under those terms.

Monks and Friars

The first means used was the development of that system of monasticism which we discussed at some length last time. Monasticism was essentially a lay and an aristocratic movement, and at this period it came to the peak of its development, its usefulness, and also of its reputation. The Benedictine system lasted for a considerable time, and, indeed, has continued to the present day. The Benedictine monks did manage to establish their monasteries throughout Europe, choosing, as likely as not, desolate spots where they were the first to introduce definite systems of agriculture, and valuable examples of culture. People sometimes wondered why the monks, like the hermits of the old days, should choose to make such outlying places the centre of their work. The answer is, partly because their culture, both of the soil and of the populace, tended to be most effective in the wilder parts. And also—and this is very often forgotten—because they believed that the evil spirits, which were driven more and more from the more popular centres, found refuge in the wilder and more desert places of the earth. So the monks went out into the very front line in order there to do battle with the most potent enemies of the Gospel, and of the Church. Their going out into these desolate places was, in itself, an act of heroism which attracted the attention of the times in which they lived.

Under the Benedictine system each one of those monasteries was independent and autonomous. Presently it was found that that opened the way for a certain amount of abuse; and there came a great reform in the monastic system towards the end of the tenth century when Cluny started the system of bringing a number of monasteries under one central head; so that when a fresh monastery was started it was not allowed to develop independently; it remained under the allegiance of the abbot of the parent house. That system of reform in monasticism spread throughout Europe and was very powerful in England. Associated with it was a determined effort to do everything possible to strengthen the power of the Papacy. Probably it was for that reason that the Papacy took more and more interest in the monastic development, and gradually secured the release of the monks from the control of the diocesan bishops, so that henceforth they should recognize the central authority of the Papacy, and should owe obedience to the Pope, and not to the local authorities on the spot.

There were other efforts to reform monasticism; as each succeeding reform died out a new one took its place. There were many varieties from the Cistercian onwards. But being in the main, as I have said, an aristocratic movement, monasticism was not able to reach the poorest people, particularly those living in the towns. In the thirteenth century, when the lot of the populace began to attract the attention of the ecclesiastical authorities, there came a tremendous new movement, an entirely fresh type of monasticism; it was not strictly speaking monasticism at all, but a fresh type of asceticism. It found its most characteristic expression in the work of the Dominican and Franciscan friars. They came with the express purpose of inaugurating a democratic movement in Christianity, bringing the Gospel into the lanes and streets of the cities, and very often outside the city walls, where there were none of the ordinary amenities of city civilization. The friars were able to do a great work in these poverty-stricken areas, and among a people who had been largely neglected. It is interesting to remember that those who began in this way also found almost immediately a fresh outlet for their energies in a quite different quarter, namely, in the Universities. Not only were the friars originally renowned for the quality of their lives, but the Orders became monuments of learning in practically all the great Universities of Europe. But whether monks or friars they did act as auxiliaries to the main pastorate, that of the parochial clergy. It is well to remember how great and intense this pastoral care really was. It is the background of all medieval life.

Medieval Unity

With that in our minds, let us try to get a picture of that unity, which is the main characteristic of the Middle Ages. In great contrast to the divisions, and highly-specialized departments of our own time, life in the Middle Ages did strive to represent itself as an unity; and I suppose it more nearly succeeded than it has ever done through the history of mankind. Unity is the outstanding characteristic of the organization, whether secular or ecclesiastical. St. Augustine, when he wrote *The City of God*, pointed out that there were two cities: one an earthly, and one a heavenly. While he did to some extent compare the earthly city with the Roman empire, and the heavenly city with the Christian Church, later ages suggested that the Holy Roman empire itself partook of a certain heavenly character, while the Christian Church had its own earthly element; so that the distinction between the two was not quite clear-cut. In later medieval thought all organization of human life was regarded as being of one piece, with two contrasted aspects. So that on one side of the shield, so to speak, you had the secular organization, and, on the other side of the shield you had the ecclesiastical organization. These two

F

were not entirely separate, but merely distinct aspects of the theocracy—the rule of God—which was meant to dominate men's hearts and lives in every respect.

There were many arguments as to who was the leading representative of this double aspect of power; and the issue was not quite as clear as we sometimes think. The Bishop of Rome claimed to be the Vicar of Christ; the Emperor also claimed to be the Vicar of Christ, although his claim is not so well-known. On the other hand, the fact that the Emperors had gone to the Pope for the recognition of their sovereignty, for their anointing and their coronation, from Charlemagne onwards, gave the lead to the ecclesiastical power. It was the *a priori* case for making it appear that the Church was the greater authority of the two. Furthermore, if the Church derived its power, as in the Middle Ages it said it did, from Peter who held the keys of Heaven, well, obviously it would seem that it had the prior claim to consideration. So there came about, very largely fostered by ecclesiastical writers, who had the habit of looking upon the Church as the sun in the heavens, while the secular power was merely the moon which shone by reason of its reflected light, the theory that all power derived from God was received, so to speak, in the first instance by the Papacy, and was transmitted only in part to the Emperor and to the people who ruled under him.

That was the theory; but in actual practice there

always was a certain tension between the ecclesiastical
and the secular powers; and over and over again you
find that the secular power is trying to release itself
from the tutelage of the ecclesiastical. That is the
essential meaning of the whole investiture controversy, a controversy that breaks out in one form or
another over and over again. But, on the whole, it
would be true to say that the Church did maintain
its supremacy, and its power was actually recognized
not only in ecclesiastical things, but also in secular
things in large measure. Ultimately it broke down
because the affairs of mankind became more and more
involved, complex, and specialized; and it was impossible for the Church effectively to supervise authority
in both spheres.

Well now, just as you get this sort of unity in organization, so you have a very marked measure of unity
in thought. The method of thought in medieval
times was entirely different from that which character-
izes our thinking to-day. If you want nowadays to
build up knowledge, what you do is to begin by
observing things; you look at things; you group things
according to their common characteristics; you
classify them, and see how they work, and thus, by
observation, you try to reach a conclusion with regard
to a whole class. So you build up your knowledge
from particulars to generals. In the medieval period
people began in exactly the opposite way. They
began with revelation which came from God; and from
that revelation they tried to deduce conclusions about

other events which came within their notice. It is well-known that in the early medieval period they followed very largely the philosophical teaching of Plato. But in the thirteenth century, under Thomas Aquinas, interest shifted from Plato to Aristotle who was more realistic. Nevertheless, the general attitude towards knowledge still remained roughly the same. Roger Bacon, in the thirteenth century, is the first to suggest to people that what they ought to do is to try to look around them, and to build up knowledge from observation, but it was a very long time before that view prevailed. It was the *a priori* method as contrasted with the *a posteriori* method that was popular. People began with generals and proceeded to reach conclusions with regard to particulars. It is an excellent method for teaching, but it is not nearly so good as the *a posteriori* method, the method of observing, of beginning with your particulars, for original research. The difficulty is if you begin with generals, and try to come by logical deductions to particulars, you may find yourself, even while you appear to be obeying the rule of the syllogism, reaching a conclusion which observation would show was entirely wrong.

You have only to contrast the quite sublime knowledge that the great scholastic teachers arrived at with regard to spiritual existence, with their really abysmal ignorance about the ordinary natural life in which they lived, which you would have thought they had every opportunity of observing for themselves. When you discover what the ordinary people of the period thought about many animals and birds, you realize how very far they could get from actual reality. The idea that the hare has as many places of conception as the years of its age; the idea that the lioness has her children stillborn, and that on the third day she roars over them and they then open their eyes and come to life; the idea that the peacock is a very good example of immortality because its flesh is incorruptible—it is extraordinary how you can get miles away from the truth by making merely 'logical' deductions without bringing them to the test of ordinary, common-sense observation.

That consideration ought to give us the means of finding an answer to the question whether the Middle Ages were really the great age of faith, or whether they were a great age of superstition. Probably the best answer is 'yes' and 'no' to both sides of the question. There was tremendous faith, a faith which was quite superb; and, at the same time, there was a great deal of credulity, and a certain amount of superstition. I think that, probably, the same sort of thing is to be said in regard to the moral standards of the Middle Ages. Were people better then than they are to-day, or worse? If you think of a man like St. Francis, you might say they were much better, because it is generally held that St. Francis is the nearest approach to the standard set by our Lord Himself that you find any-where among the biographies of human beings. On the other hand, you have to recognize that people were extraordinarily cruel to each other; and that they were even more cruel to animals. For our own age we should have said that that would have been impossible if we had not gone through the horrors of two world wars, which have left as an aftermath a greater amount of cruelty than we have seen for many generations. But apart from the influence of war, it would be true to say that cruelty, in any shape or form, revolts us as a nation, whereas in the Middle Ages it would be taken as a matter of course.

One of the difficulties about estimating the moral standard of the Middle Ages is the fact that while we live our lives in the terms of one moral standard for everybody, they took it for granted that there were two standards, one standard for the monk, who sacrificed the possibility of home-life in order to give himself to the service of God; and another for ordinary Christians. If you preferred, or felt you were called, to stay in the world, then an entirely different standard was demanded of you from that of the monk; and a great deal was possible and proper for you that was not either possible, or proper, for the monk. And that does not apply merely to the monastic rule but to the whole sphere of practical Christianity. The people of the Middle Ages did regard it as part of the inherited Christian ideal that there should be two different standards, one for the ascetic, and the other for the ordinary person living in the world. The monk must be quite literally a *better* man than the ordinary Christian. Monasticism was itself the essential

Christianity. Some scholars suggest that that really is the solution of our difficulties; that we ought to have, and to recognize, a double standard. I should disagree there. Instinctively we must all feel that there can be only one standard for everybody; but we recognize that one standard does not mean that we have all got to do the same things, and all show the same self-sacrifice. The one standard, surely, for everybody is to do whatever is the will of God for him. What we have to do is to try to discover what God wants each one of us to do, and then to do it. There is the ideal for everybody. God may be calling one person to be a monk, another a priest; He may be calling one to live out of the world, and another to live in the world. That is something that each one must find out for himself; find out his true calling, and then be true to it. In that sense there is only one standard. There may be millions of different paths along the same level, but there are not two levels in Christianity. I do not regard the medieval solution of the moral question as satisfactory.

There is one other thing about this general medieval picture to which I would draw attention, and that is its tremendous artistic achievement. The thirteenth century was the greatest century the world has ever known. Its greatness appears in the varied character of the advances that were made, but I suppose that nowhere is its achievement more conspicuous than in the realm of architecture. It is in the medieval period that we get the full flower of Gothic architecture.

The old Romanesque about which we were talking last time disappeared, and in its place you get this light and aspiring type of architecture which we know as Gothic. How it came to be developed is a secret which is not really completely known even to the greatest pundits. But the essential thing was the discovery of the pointed arch. It resulted in a complete revolution in architecture. Buildings became much higher and lighter. No longer did the master masons need these great, massive walls to support the weight of the roof and superstructure. All that could be carried without much wall at all, the arches receiving the thrust and directing it down to the pillars; and the pillars proving capable of supporting the whole structure. Buttresses left them free to leave out much of the walls between the pillars and to fill in the space with glass. Some people have thought that one of the reasons why this style was developed was because the towns were getting more and more cramped, and there was not a large amount of space in them. Just as in New York the people have had to find accommodation, when they could not spread their buildings wide over the ground, by pushing them up into the air, so the Gothic building might be described as a kind of sky-scraper edition of the early church building. That is one explanation of the way in which this new type of architecture came in. Having come in it did provide the world with the most glorious example of the builder's art that it has ever known. It is in the full flower of the Gothic architecture, with its magnificent lightness, its aspiring reaches, and its general sense of daring and courage, that we have the best symbol of the heroic quality of the Middle Ages.

Renaissance

Now it seems a terrible tragedy that all that unity should break down, but break down it did. The change, when it came, was due to a change in people's method of thinking. It came about when people began to get interested in the old Greek literature, and to recapture something of the freedom of spirit that was characteristic of the great age in Greek thought. We generally symbolize it by saying it was all due to the capture of Constantinople by the Turks in 1453, and the sending of Greek manuscripts out into Europe for everybody to read. Actually the dissemination of Greek ideas had been going on long before that. It was coming to a point then, and it was developed most tremendously in Italy. There it produced a new Humanism in which people began to realize more than ever before of how much man was capable. Fresh horizons opened out before them. People like Leonardo da Vinci were beginning to realize what man could do if he set himself to look at things in a scientific way.

At the same time people were beginning to make more adventures across the seas than ever before; they were discovering new countries; new horizons were opening up everywhere. They really began to think what wonderful people they were. 'If only we can live up to our own capacity there is really nothing we cannot do.' And they began to be drunk with the ecstasy of their own achievements. And by centring their thought upon this, regarding man as the maker of things, they began to feel they ought to be subject to no restraint. The new interest in life which came in with the Greek literature began to develop in them a new interest in physical life, and eventually it began to deteriorate into an inordinate desire for low and sensual pleasures. What took place in Italy at that time is very like the Humanism which is re-developing in our own day. The new worlds man has conquered to-day are in the air, in the region of science and in the sphere of mechanical inventions. Once again he has become impatient of traditional views and of traditional restraints, and we are witnessing something like a violent revolution in the moral sphere. Well, you had something of that same sort at the end of the medieval period.

Even the hierarchy was affected by the moral landslide. That is the reason why in Rome and in Italy you find so many of the senior clergy whose lives will not bear inspection. Seriousness seems almost to have disappeared from life in Italy. That was not true of the northern countries. There the new Humanism took an entirely different form. The interest in Greek literature, so far as the northern countries are concerned, became concentrated upon the sacred books, and it expressed itself in a new interest in the New Testament. As people began to learn Greek, and were able to read the New Testament in its original language, they also began to learn Hebrew and were able to read the Old Testament in its original language. So in the north the Renaissance took on a more serious turn. You can see the contrast between the two types if you compare Machiavelli with the Oxford Reformers—Colet, More, and Erasmus.

Machiavelli is a patriot, and he wants to give advice about the best system of Government. And he says: 'How do things stand? How can we turn them best to our own particular purpose?' As he examines the question he takes the view that people are governed more by fear than by love; and he says 'If you want to rule them you must use the fear motive and not the love motive.' And from that particular point he evolves the whole of this theory concerning the system of government; and the result is that the name of Machiavelli has become associated with the worst kind of tyranny, and with all that is bad in the art of government. When his ideas were revived by Mussolini and by Hitler, we said: 'What can we expect when men go back to teaching of that kind!' The Christian tradition had been so undermined that Machiavelli had no true moral basis for the theories he developed.

On the other hand, in the Oxford reformers, Colet, More, and Erasmus, you get a change of thought which is still in line with the definitely Christian view of morality. Everything they can learn from St. Paul and from the rest of the New Testament they try to turn to the benefit of a fuller understanding of life and its implications. There you have a picture of people of the most definitely serious intent, who have not lost their faith in God or in humanity, people who hold that love is still the guiding principle of life. They recognize the abuses in the Church but think they can easily be remedied through the spread of the new learning. However, the deterioration of the Church had gone so far that it was very unlikely that many would have been satisfied with the palliatives proposed by people like Colet, More, and Erasmus. If the Church had not been so thoroughly degraded, the Oxford reformers might have carried it along new paths of progress. But it was not to be; more violent measures were necessary before people were satisfied that they had got to the heart of things.

The Reformation

When we move on to the Reformation period we see how the state of things affected a man like Luther, with an intensely emotional temperament and a passionate longing for salvation. He felt that religion had been prostituted to the most sordid ends, and nowhere did he see that more graphically portrayed than in the case of Tetzel, the friar who came round selling indulgences. Luther had tried to attain to purity of character and a guarantee of eternal security as a true son of the Church, but he had found himself fail in the effort, until he had been led, while still in the monastery, to realize that whatever may be the rules and regulations there is at the heart of the Christian religion only one thing possible, and that is to realize the love of Christ, and the forgiveness that love has brought.

Luther, having gone through that experience, found himself face to face with a person like Tetzel whose indulgences were going to pay for the building of St. Peter's at Rome after the Archbishop of Mainz had been allowed to take his share of the proceeds to reimburse himself for the money spent on getting into his See. People were to be freed from the consequences, both temporal and eternal, of their sins if they put sufficient money into the box. That is putting the case in regard to these indulgences, as Luther saw it; I am still not putting it as crudely as Tetzel himself did. There was not a thinking person who did not see how far this business was removed from essential Christianity. And a person of Luther's strong emotional temperament could not possibly face a situation of that kind without revolting. In 1517 he nailed up his 95 Theses which were intended to be a basis of discussion against this way of doing things. When he found that he was not able to obtain redress, he carried the thing further, and presently you find that the whole of Europe is in a ferment. Luther was not a great theologian; he was a religious genius, a great preacher and a wonderful pamphleteer, but he was not able to systematize his beliefs, nor was he able to propound any adequate theory of the Church. Consequently the effective control of the Reformation in Germany was gradually taken over by the civil authority; and in the Lutheran system the essential power passes from the Church into the hands of the secular rulers.

Quite a different solution was being propounded by a more statesmanlike man, Calvin, who was a systematic theologian, and a great organizer. He could organize thought, and he could organize government, and he did both in Geneva. The Calvinistic system is derived from the supreme sovereignty of God, a sovereignty which can predestine human souls to eternal life or eternal damnation, and though removed from any contact with the base material of this world, can be caught, so to speak, and reflected in a theocratic organization. That theocratic organization Calvin proceeded to evolve and put into effect. He set up that whole system which has made Presbyterianism far and away the most effective rival of Catholic theology, because it is the only system which for clarity and coherence can stand comparison with the old historical theology of the Christian Church. It issued in a Puritanism which matched the morality of Medievalism with a grim sternness expressed in terms of the Old Testament. Life in Geneva was certainly no more free than life in the medieval period. In fact, it was subject to more definite tyranny. Death was the punishment for adultery; fornication was often punished by drowning. A child was beheaded because it struck its parents. One need not continue the horrible list. This dour, stern, cold, tyrannical idea of religion arose out of the theory of God as the aloof Sovereign, and the love, and tenderness, and beauty, and gentleness of Jesus simply disappeared from view altogether.

Luther—Calvin—and then you have Zwingli, who almost gets rid of theology altogether. He takes what some people think is the layman's view of religion. He tries to rob it of all mystery. The Sacraments are nothing except just pictures, empty symbols. Christology, and theories about the nature of God—they are all mysteries, which must be carefully emptied of their content in order that in the end you may have a religion which can satisfy the cold reason of the ordinary business man. As a matter of fact, it defeats its own purpose, because the ultimate hunger in the heart of man is for religion; and a religion which is not mysterious is not a religion at all. So Zwingli could never make any great appeal except to the coldly intellectual.

Conclusion

Let me point out in conclusion that what I here have been working up to is to make it clear that the medieval system had become top-heavy; it was full of details which really did obscure the original Gospel. Also its genius had become too authoritarian; it clamped down the spirit of enquiry which was the most significant feature of the times. Only that religion could satisfy man which offered him definite freedom. 'Jerusalem which is above is free, which is the mother of us all.' 'We are not children of the bond-woman, but of the free.' The crash that came at the end of the medieval period was the result of this struggle for freedom. So we have another example of the Christian Church trying to find a fresh sphere of salvation: salvation not in this case simply of the individual, of the nation, or of culture, but salvation of freedom itself.

V

THE ANGLICAN SYNTHESIS

THE peculiar character of the English Reformation arises very largely out of the peculiar character and circumstances of Henry the Eighth. (I do not know in the least why that should arouse laughter!) Henry the Eighth was a very great man, one of the greatest monarchs that ever sat on the throne of England, and a man for whom we ought to have considerable regard. I know, of course, that many of you nowadays see him through the character portrayed by Charles Laughton; but I assure you that there is a great deal more in him than that; and that is saying a good deal. Henry the Eighth was very concerned about the succession to his throne, and he realized that he must have a son. He believed that he was not going to have a son because there was something wrong about his marriage, and, therefore, he must get that marriage annulled. He was not asking for a divorce; he was asking for a declaration of nullity in order that he might achieve his ambition, and, through another marriage, get a male heir to his throne. There would normally have been in the state of thought and temper of the time no difficulty about that. Unfortunately for him, because there had been a doubt about the marriage from the start, everything had been done to tie it up as tightly as possible; and when it came to the question of untying, the Pope was under the thumb of the nephew of the wife whose marriage was to be declared null and void; and it was extremely difficult to give the king his heart's desire. Thus, in order to achieve his object, Henry had to dismiss the Pope, so to speak, get rid of the Papacy, and find another authority which would recognize the grounds for his re-marriage. That was not the cause of the Reformation in England, but it was the occasion for the Reformation to take place. There would certainly have been a Reformation, whatever may have been the character of the king, or the circumstances of his reign; but it so happened that this particular situation occasioned the split with the Papacy and gave opportunity for the rise of the Movement in England.

Now Henry was a theologian. Do not forget that he had been originally destined for the chair of St. Augustine at Canterbury; and, as a theologian, he knew what was the religious situation. He had not the slightest intention of letting the country follow the lines of the Continental Reformation. He did not want a revolution in theology; in fact, what he wanted was Catholicism without the Pope; and that he proceeded to give to his country as far as he could. The fruits of his policy, as a matter of fact, are to be seen to a large extent in the first Prayer Book of the following reign. The English Prayer Book of 1549 is a most admirable Book, which does achieve a very large measure of

Henry's ambition in the way of theology, while expressing, at the same time, the genius of one of the greatest writers of English prose our literature has known. It gave us a very splendid liturgy; it gave us a choir office which should have become extremely popular; it made proper provision for the occasional offices; it inaugurated an intelligible reading of the Scriptures. In short, I think it is the best Book that we have actually produced.

It would have been a very admirable thing if its compilers could have fixed Anglicanism somewhere about that level. But it could not be done because Henry had in the meantime set another example which was of the very worst kind. He had dissolved the monasteries—one of the worst things he ever did. I am not going to defend the monasteries. Monasticism had gone out of fashion; it had ceased to do its best work; and it had been replaced very largely in the affection of the charitable by the schools and Universities. There is no doubt at all that some of the monasteries, and particularly the smaller ones, were not worth keeping. Nevertheless, there was none of the wholesale corruption that people talk about to-day; and it is a thousand pities that disaster should have overwhelmed an institution which had done such valuable work in the history of the Christian Church, and which has been revived once again to-day in order to meet a fundamental need. But Henry wanted money, and that was the means Thomas Cromwell used of getting it for him.

He set an example, an example which the uncles of Edward the Sixth were quite ready to follow. They realized that if they could let the Reformation change to Continental lines, then they would undermine the reason for the great possessions and wealth of the Church. So I am afraid they did proceed quite cynically to do just that. Without any strong theological interest of their own, they pushed the Reformation along extremist lines in order that they might rob the Church for their own advantage. The result of that is seen in the Prayer Book of 1552 which represents the English Church at its nearest approach to Puritanism. But it did not last long, and I doubt whether the 1552 Prayer Book was ever widely used in this country.

Edward the Sixth was followed by Queen Mary; and the country was extremely glad to see her, because it was tired of the rapacity and the mismanagement of the former reign . . . Mary came with the prospect of a return to normality in religion. The people thought, 'At any rate, here would be some one who would respect the Church, and religious organizations in general.' Poor woman! Her life is one of the greatest tragedies in English history; we need not go into it now; but she did succeed in disappointing every hope that was held of her reign. People began to associate her particular religion with the fires of Smithfield, with the resuscitation of that bullying character which has always expressed itself through the institutions that come from Italy.

By the time Mary's reign was over, the people were

more tired of the religion she represented than they
had been of the religion represented by Edward the
Sixth's uncles. Both types were heartily abhorred by
the bulk of the people in the country; and when
Elizabeth came to the throne, representing the possibility of some moderation, some *via media*, some
settlement in religion, then the country, as a whole,
leapt to welcome her, and to forward her efforts.
Every one knows that in her own practice Elizabeth
was what we nowadays call a High Churchwoman.
She would, I think, if she could, have gone straight
back to the position at the end of the reign of Henry
the Eighth, but, failing that, she did the best she
could; and she encouraged the Church to regard its
own interests, and to manage its own organization. She
tried to see that it had sufficient means to carry on its
work; she was very insistent upon the dignity of its
worship; she was anxious that it should not lean too
much upon her, or upon the State. The Prayer Book
of 1559 was the result. It did not go so far as to
reproduce the 1549 Prayer Book as a whole, but it
represented the best that could be done in that
direction.

Roughly, things have remained as they were fixed
at that time. The Elizabethan settlement, on the whole,
still remains the position of the English Church.
There were, of course, various schisms, because,
welcome as was this settlement of Elizabeth's, there
were certain bodies of people who were not prepared
to accept it. They are all rather tragic because they all

arise out of a very sincere endeavour to restore what their founders believed to be the original system of Christianity as exhibited in the pages of Scripture. Actually, for the first time, the Scriptures had been laid open for people to read. From Cranmer's Bible in 1538 to the Authorised Version in 1611 various succeeding editions were made open to the public. Where the Scriptures were too expensive for people to buy privately, they were to be found chained in the churches, and people could read them there. This reading of the Bible was a complete astonishment to the people. Their first reaction to it was—'This is not the least bit like the Church we have known.' The old medievalism had incorporated a great deal which was not Christian at all, but sub-Christian; and that was something which they could not find in the pages of Scripture. They began to ask themselves, 'What can we do in order to get back to primitive Christianity?' But they had, first of all, to make up their minds what primitive Christianity really was. And when you come to think of it, that is a question that we have been asking ever since. Some of us have given a lifetime to the study of the subject, and we are not yet in complete agreement as to what primitive Christianity really was. If that is true of us you can imagine what confusion there was in the minds of people then who had not our background of scholarship, nor our opportunity of research, but who simply tried to interpret the situation as they found it set out for them in the pages of Scripture. As a result many different types of organization arose, all of which neglected the whole of the history of the period between the primitive age and their own day, and simply tried to take a leap back to the first century. It was, as I have already pointed out, very largely Henry's own theological knowledge which prevented us doing anything of the kind. The English Church did refuse to accept a solution which would mean the complete jettisoning of the intervening centuries between the first and the sixteenth. That was the real difference between her and the sects.

It is from that point you get the emergence of what we may call Anglicanism. You get it in Parker and in Jewel, and most definitely of all in Hooker. A book which Hallam said was the first great prose work in our language, and which Pope Clement said had within it the seeds of eternity, was Hooker's treatise *Of the Laws of Ecclesiastical Polity*. One can say that here was a work which was calculated to make the whole contemporary Christendom realize that there was a new power in Europe with which theologians must make some sort of terms. Actually it did prove effective to some of the brightest minds on the Continent, both on the Reformed side and also on the Catholic side, and it won a number of converts. But England was not now very much concerned with what happened on the Continent; nor did it attempt to proselytize there. It was satisfied with finding its own solution within its own boundaries, and there it did try to maintain a religion free from abuses which had come down through the centuries from the time of our Lord. That religion in its Anglican form was reformed; nevertheless, it was Catholic in the sense that it preserved its connection with past history and was continuous with the religion of the first century.

The Enlightenment

That kind of religion, having thus started its career, soon found itself endeavouring to express itself definitely and clearly against a background of thought which became less and less sympathetic. Curiously enough, it was in this country that there first developed a distinction between a revealed religion, on the one hand, and what was called a natural religion, on the other. Under leading philosophers like Locke and Hobbes, people began to pay tremendous attention to reason as apart from revelation. Coupled with that was the growth of scientific thought. At last men began to realize that you cannot force upon nature *a priori* conclusions, but that you must try to observe nature, and learn from her. That definite development of scientific thought, combined with the emphasis upon reason, led people to try to find a sort of least common multiple behind all the religions of the world. They were getting to know a little about Confucianism, and various pagan religions; they were beginning to see how much of value there was in the philosophical and moral teaching of the great sages of the world; and they thought it would be a very fine thing if they could find a common denominator of all those religions and philosophies. On that they could be united and they could get rid of the dogmas, whether Papist or Protestant, that had done so much to divide society.

That teaching spread from England to France where it was picked up by Voltaire, and developed into a philosophy of life which was—not atheistic— but rather deistic. They were quite ready to admit the existence of God, so long as He was not concerned too much with this world, and did not interfere; so long as they could carry on their reasoning, and take no notice of that particular hypothesis. They required a God in the background because they did try to establish a moral law; and that was hard to maintain on any other hypothesis. Also to justify the moral law they required belief in a future life. Here we see the righteous very often neglected; therefore there must be an immortality in which righteousness will have its proper reward. That was the position taken by Voltaire; and with more avowed scepticism by Frederick the Great in Germany. In that country it lent itself to a re-examination of the Christian documents. People had been accustomed to accept the Bible as something which had fallen from Heaven, so to speak, and which must be accepted as it stood, and could not be examined too closely. You must not submit it to the same kind of research to which you would submit any ordinary document; that would be an act of sacrilege. But under the impetus of this new type of thought people lost that fear, and they put the Bible to very careful examination. They found that if you exam-

H

ined it as carefully as that, you could see very good reason for regarding its literary history and composition as being on a par with that of the literature of any civilized country; and they submitted the Bible to the same kind of historical investigation as that to which they would submit any other literary anthology.

The influence of this deistic type of thought meant, to a very large extent, the evaporation of distinctive religious feeling. The warmth of love for Christ disappeared out of religion, particularly among the Lutherans in Germany, but also elsewhere. The eighteenth century is very largely characterized by this arid, barren type of religion which emphasizes the 'natural' at the expense of the 'revealed' elements in religion.

The Non-Jurors

If now we get back again to England, we can see what efforts were made to disentangle people from the effects of this particular kind of thought. In the first place there was one which occurred even before the eighteenth century, made by the people known as the Non-Jurors. It began in 1690. It arose originally out of a refusal of a number of the bishops to accept William the Third after the abdication of James the Second. Earlier James had put some of them into prison because they had opposed the unconstitutional use of the royal prerogative. But, in spite of that fact, when William came over, they would not break their oath of allegiance to James, and held that it was still binding upon them. It was a difficult situation. In our day we think of the monarchy as being bound up with the law; but they did not; they relied entirely upon the theory of divine right. If James was by divine right king of this country, then no one had any right to displace him. If he proved unworthy, then you must bow your head, and suffer patiently; passive obedience was your duty, and you must not, by any means whatsoever, turn your back upon him. Well, that is what they felt. And, rather than take the oath of allegiance to William and Mary they were prepared to go out into the wilderness.

Eight Bishops, with four hundred of the Clergy, did go out, and form a schism. In some ways, it was a disaster for the nation, because it took out of the Church of England at that critical period some of the best elements in it, including the saintly Bishop Ken. It was a sad loss to the National Church. Not only so, it was a loss to theology; because it so happened that these people, with their exalted notion of kingship, were most interested in the historical side of theological studies; and that was the side that was very badly needed to assist the whole ecclesiastical atmosphere that was developing at that period. On the other hand, William the Third, with his Dutch Calvinism, was not really in sympathy with the English Church. He did not understand its history—and very few people have done so—but William did not really know it; and he bent all his weight against its distinctive character. On the other hand, it may be said that the Non-Jurors, having their hands freed of all the multifarious obligations that rested upon the national clergy, were now able to develop their own liturgy along their own lines, and to carry the Catholic element in Anglicanism to a more logical conclusion than was possible in the Established Church. At any rate, it is quite true, whichever way you look at it, that the work done by the Non-Jurors did have a great deal of effect upon the later thought and development of Anglicanism, and acted as a defensive barrier against the corrosive influence of Deism.

The Methodists

Another effort to resist the dead weight of deistic thought was found in a very different quarter, namely, among a few undergraduates at Oxford, who were giving themselves to good works, visiting the prisoners in the prisons, caring for the poor in the poorer parts of the town, and meeting together for regular worship and exercise of one kind and another, and who were profoundly interested in all sorts of ecclesiastical questions. They were led by two brothers, John and Charles Wesley. And because they had a rather High Church attitude towards religion, and kept the rules and regulations of the Church very carefully, they were called Methodists. That essentially High Church movement did eventually turn into the Evangelical Revival. It introduced into this country a heart religion, a religion of the inner conscience, which was very refreshing, and very alive, as contrasted with the dull apathy of the more characteristic religion of the day.

I would not like any one to run away with the idea that in the eighteenth century the whole of the English Church was given over to the deistic type of religion. Very gallant efforts were being made by the leaders of the National Church throughout that period to save essential Christianity from the corroding influence of deistic thought. What they were contending for were not the niceties of religious faith and practice, but the essentials of Christian doctrine: faith in God, as not merely transcendent, but also immanent; faith in the Incarnation, that Jesus is, after all, the Son of God. That defence of the Christian faith was put up by people who were the leaders of thought in the English Church. The greatest of them was Bishop Butler, who in his *Analogy* effected a tremendous defence of essential Christianity, and more especially of essential Christian morals. So do not let people persuade you that in the eighteenth century there was nothing but apathy in the National Church. That is quite a wrong view to take. And not only men like Butler, working on an academic level, but also the parochial clergy in the parishes were doing a work of tremendous value. They did more than look after the souls of their parishioners; they looked after their bodies also. Very often they acted as amateur doctors of the district and ministered to the ailing people in the country places. Their wives knew all about the needs of sick people, and carried nursing comforts into the cottages of the poor. And together, husbands and wives, did a work of real practical effect, before anything like State Welfare Work had been thought of. Nearly all the Welfare Work of those days was in the hands of these hard-working parsons in the parishes. All that needs to be remembered when we are thinking about the eighteenth century.

Nevertheless, there was a cold, conventional respectability which dominated the scene. And, as always, in a situation of that kind, some one will, sooner or later, sound a signal of revolt, and will try to lead people away from the purely intellectual apprehension to a religion which warms the heart. Some one will say: 'It is all very well; unless you are really converted you cannot be a true follower of Jesus Christ.' It was that which John and Charles Wesley brought into the religious life of the eighteenth century. They did insist that people must be converted to Christ. Their idea of conversion, owing to the particular results of their own preaching, led them to regard it as being necessarily accompanied by a good deal of emotional excitement. Indeed, the scenes at some of the preachments of John Wesley must have been almost unbelievable by people who had never seen anything like it before. Certainly they were very shocking to the academic temperament of the eighteenth century and the Bishops were revolted by such 'enthusiasm'.

But John Wesley was not the only one who had this tremendous influence. A person who was, in some ways, even a greater preacher, with a stronger effect upon his audience, was George Whitefield. He had been a friend of the Wesleys at the University; he had been a poor servitor at Pembroke College, Oxford, and then had been ordained. When he began his preaching he worked in harmony with the Wesleys, but later he developed a theology quite unlike theirs. The Wesleys were what was called Arminian, believing that the most precious thing in our possession is our freedom of will, so that we can determine whether we will do good or evil. Whitefield followed the Calvinistic theology which taught that people were not free to choose good or evil, eternal life or eternal damnation: all was pre-determined by God. The difference between the two theological outlooks led to a split. John Wesley, who had a far greater genius for organization than White-field, and who, by the way, was a very strong autocrat, developed his own particular organization. Every one knows the story of the way in which, thoroughly impatient at not being able to get his scheme accepted, and failing to get bishops consecrated for the work in America, he ventured to consecrate a bishop him-self. And so was started the great Methodist Episcopal Church in America, involving ultimately a break-away from the Church of England.

On the other hand, Whitefield, with his Calvinistic type of theology, remained in the English Church; and he was responsible for that particular type of thought which, in our Church, is known as Evan-gelical. Evangelicalism to-day has departed a good deal from Whitefield's Calvinistic type of theology:

nevertheless, that is the basis of it. It is interesting to note that although, in some ways, Wesley was much more essentially Anglican than Whitefield, his followers left the Church of England; while Whitefield, with his more Calvinistic theology, which was not so near the centre of Anglican thought, remained within it.

Oxford Movement

The Evangelical Revival was followed at the beginning of the nineteenth century by the Catholic Revival. In Oxford under Keble, Pusey, and Newman a new movement was started which emphasized the churchly aspect of religion. It insisted just as strongly as the Wesleys did upon the personal nature of religion, but it laid much greater stress upon the Church as a Divine Society, and even more than the Wesleys, it insisted upon the necessity of a continued struggle for holiness of personal life. I emphasize this last point because it is so often neglected in accounts of the Catholic Revival. The really essential thing in the movement was the struggle for personal holiness. You find it in Keble, in Pusey, and in Newman; and you cannot understand the genius of the movement unless you get hold of that particular thought.

But what has captured the imagination still more is the insistence its leaders laid upon the churchly aspect of religion. They were incensed at the way in which the State had impinged upon the work of the Church. They felt that the Church was becoming more and more cramped within the claws of the State; that the State was presuming to dictate to the people in religious matters without recognizing that this was really the concern of the Church itself. Out of this quite practical reaction they developed against current views of the Establishment the doctrine of the independent position of the Church, and its historical character, which was particularly guaranteed by the apostolic succession of its ministers. They evolved a 'branch' theory of the divisions of the Christian Church as a body, showing how it had come down as one unit through its early history, dividing later into two branches, East and West, in the eleventh century, and then putting forth a new branch from the West, called Anglicanism, in the sixteenth century. They believed that in these three branches of the Church there was the guarantee of a definite continuity. They did not seem to realize that exactly the same claim could have been put forward for the Lutheran Church in Sweden, a fact which was brought home to the English Church later under the influence of John Wordsworth, Bishop of Salisbury. So here you have Keble, and Pusey, and Newman emphasizing the churchly aspect of Anglicanism, and, consequently, emphasizing the belief that saving grace is guaranteed and conveyed through the ordinances of the Church, so long as those ordinances have been preserved intact. That is what gave strength to their movement. People were lifted out of the belief that they had, in any sort of way, to yield to the dictates of the State in religious matters. They realized that the Church had a continuous history, from the time it was founded upon the apostles and prophets to the present day. In other words, it was an organization which could ensure to people a realization of the fact that God is not right away beyond the farthest star, and that Jesus is not One who lived two thousand years back in history, but that they are here now, and we in the Christian Church are actually incorporated into the Saviour, and made one with Him. From that view, of course, there followed a great deal of interest in the minor details of Church organization and worship. The result of that Movement has been that it has actually revolutionized the manner of worship throughout the whole length and breadth of the Anglican Communion. How far it has penetrated below those external details, and got into the hearts and lives of people it would be very difficult to say. Nevertheless, it is true that in each one of these movements, whether Non-Juror, or Evangelical, or Tractarian, there has always been this effort to win people away from a merely intellectual or formal presentation of Christianity, and to make them realize that they can get into touch with a living Saviour here and now, and that progress must start, so to speak, from the point where they are conscious that they have come into an attitude of friendship and love with Him.

The Anglican Synthesis

Well now, you will, I hope, perceive from what I have tried to say what my view of the Anglican Synthesis is. Let us remember, first of all, that we do stand or fall by the fact that we have tried to effect a synthesis. We have accepted the historical implications of the continuity of the Christian Church. We have accepted also a large measure of the new thought which has come into Christendom in succeeding ages. We have also accepted the view of the Evangelical leaders that religion must be a matter of the heart, and not mere conformity of conduct. We have tried to incorporate into our own tradition these different strains. We hold out one hand to the Churches of the pre-Reformation period; and we hold out the other to the Churches of the post-Reformation period. We have certain contacts with them both. Our particular difficulty is this: that at the present time, within our own Church, the traditions which bind us together in this Anglican synthesis have expressed themselves in greater extremes. I am sorry to have to use the word 'extremes' but I cannot think of any other word to use at the moment. We have pushed these tendencies further than we have ever done before, whether it be on the side of Catholicism, or whether it be on the side of Evangelicalism. We have pulled each strand of our common heritage further in our own generation than any element in the National Church has done since the Anglican settlement was first conceived. The question is whether we can maintain our unity under this new, and as many people think, this excessive strain. Personally, I believe that, under the guidance of God, we are being led to test the different qualities in the strands which combine to make up our united being to their utmost limit. I doubt whether it is possible to go further. We have reached the bound of experiment. I have no doubt at all, that, in the providence of God, we shall achieve a new stage exhibiting the old synthesis at a higher level, with an even richer content. If we realize what the Anglican Communion really is, a Communion depending for its *raison d'être* upon this synthesis which, under the guidance of God, was established at the very outset if its distinct existence; if we realize that, then I think we have very good hope for the future. And it seems to me that it would be, not merely a thousand pities, but a disaster of the first magnitude, if we did not combine together to achieve this new stage. Because, surely, at the present time, there is no Christian Communion which has anything like the opportunities that we have of assisting in the re-union of the scattered members of the Church of Christ throughout the world. Surely, if there is any body of Christians called out by God to assist in the Re-union of Christendom, it is the Anglican Communion.

I remember once saying that in the course of some University Extension Lectures. And afterwards a young man came up to me, and said, 'I was interested in what you said; but you are not the only people, you know. I am a Swede, and we say exactly the same thing about ourselves in Sweden.' I was very interested to hear him say that, because it shows that thought can move along the same lines even in countries which have had little theological connection with each other. As a matter of fact, in recent years, we have had those from Sweden who have been very familiar with our English and Anglican character. It so happens that the best history of the Oxford Movement, *The Catholic Revival*, was written by a Swede, Yngve Brilioth. And it is well to remember that the National Church of Sweden, like ourselves, preserved its historical continuity at the Reformation without a break, and that it is in communion with us to-day. We do not want to claim any exclusive privileges for ourselves. There are others who value this point of view, and are prepared to develop the same synthesis. And we shall be only too glad to accept their help, and to extend our help to them. What we have to make clear to our own generation is that we are not trying to combine two opposing traditions: two mutually exclusive religions. Like the writers of the New Testament, we may each have our own way of presenting the scheme of salvation; but we are united in the same creed, the same ministry, the same sacraments. We rest upon the assumption that there is no essential conflict between Catholicism and Evangelicalism. And it is when you get the best spirit of both combined that you have the strongest expression of Christianity, and the truest expression of Anglicanism. The spirit of Church history will then be most finely exemplified, when the salvation of freedom has received its complement in the salvation of unity.